dedicated to everyone who wishes they could just leave it all behind...

MW01043249

about lucinda's list

map & directory

overview

travel tips

contents

gourmet restaurant reviews

casual restaurant reviews

beach bar reviews

lolo reviews

hotels, activities, etc.

LUCINDA'S LIST
GUIDEBOOK COMPANY

about lucinda's list

A fter a two month vacation in St. Martin, my husband and I did what so many people swear they're going to do. We decided to leave our old lives, careers and plans behind to make a new life traveling & writing about the islands of the Caribbean.

LUCINDA'S LIST
GUIDEBOOK COMPANY

Managing Editors
Lucinda Newcomb
Steve Newcomb

Writing & Editing Staff
Lucinda Newcomb
Vicki Frink (Grey Squirrel)
Madam J

Creative Design
Steve Newcomb

Travelers & Tasters
Lucinda Newcomb
Steve Newcomb
Vicki Frink

Chief Drinkers
The Entire Frink/Newcomb
Family

Staff Critters
Apollo "Mr. Bean"
Belly Belle Belle

Chief Mispeller
Steve Newcomb

Stunt Doubles
Steve & Lucinda did all of
their own stunts, however
ridiculous

Photography
Lucinda Newcomb
Steve Newcomb
Madam J
Marc Au Marc

© 2010 Lucinda's List Inc.
first print 2010

http:www.lucindaslist.com

Legal disclaimer:
Although all details in this
document are based on
information supplied to us
or gathered by us at press
time, changes occur all
the time in the travel
world, especially with
restaurants, and Lucinda's
List cannot accept
responsibility for facts or
circumstances that
become outdated or for
inadvertent errors or
omissions. So always
confirm information when
it matters.

The Story of Steve & Lucinda

In Fall 2009, my husband Steve and I thought we had it all figured out. Beautiful house in Berkeley, CA, the requisite yellow lab, great technology careers... and I was pregnant. Then the fourth miscarriage hit. It broke our hearts. We needed time to heal. A break. From everything.

Seeking comfort in the form of sun, sand and food, we elected to hunker down in St. Martin for a couple months and hope for the best. It worked. We lived in the moment and ate like gods. We over-indulged. We bronzed ourselves well past the recommended allowance, letting the warmth heal us. We met joyful people pursuing non-traditional lives... and realized life doesn't have to be linear.

I started blogging. I'd always wanted to be a travel writer, ever since my first backpacking adventures in Europe almost 20 years ago, but I was too chicken. The blog began simply as a way to keep my family and friends updated so they would stop emailing me (I mean, what part of "break" didn't they understand?), and then I fell in love with recounting the stories of our day-to-day adventures.

Then what? Instead of returning home and falling back into old patterns, the life built around starting a family, I walked into my steady corporate job... and quit. To say I was terrified doesn't begin to convey my trepidation.

I started writing. For a couple months my husband and I toyed with our web site, then we created a Facebook fan page, and all of a sudden we had 25,000 fans. Huh. We might be on to something. So we decided to publish a guide - the kind of guide we wished we'd found before we went to St. Martin.

What's so different about our guide?

Consistent - Every review is written by me, or a very short list of people I explicitly know and trust, which means it's from a reliable source (if I do say so myself). There's no wading through tens of opinions, wondering which one to believe. You can compare apples to apples.

Independent - No one pays us to include them in our guidebooks, nor have we received kickbacks or payment of any kind. Even though we could probably mooch tons of freebies, we don't tell the restaurant who we are - we go in "Secret Squirrel" style. We experience each destination for real, just like you.

In-depth - Unlike most guidebooks that give you just a quick sentence or two, we go the extra mile, assessing the restaurant for everything from taste and innovativeness to atmosphere and service. We tell you everything you need to know to make an informed decision.

St. Martin is just the beginning of our adventures. This guide is our labor of love, and we hope you enjoy it.

N7

Saint Martin

Marigot

Quartier D'Orléans

Union Rd

L.B. Scott Rd

Sint Maarten

Simpson Bay

Philipsburg

map & directory

W hat good is it knowing where to go if you can't find it? Or can't call to make a reservation? We never found a decent map or restaurant directory of Grand Case during our trip, so we decided to make our own.

map & directory

LUCINDA'S LIST
GUIDEBOOK COMPANY

Grand Case, St. Martin

St. Marten/St. Martin

Anse Marcel

A

Cul-de-Sac

Grand-Case

Rambaud Quartier D'Orléans

Les Terres Basses

Sandy Ground

Marigot

Dutch Cul de Sac

Lower Prince's Quarter

Lowlands

Cole Bay

Simpson Bay

Little Bay Philipsburg

Legend

Restaurant

Hotel

Beach

Diving

Parking

Grocery

Le Ti Pr

Sky's the Limit

Talk of the Town

Il Nettuno

Le Soleil

B

Fish Pot

l'Auber

Le Tastevin

La Villa

Boulevard d Grande Case

L'Escapade

Le Cottage

La California

Piazza Pascal

s des Écoles

Pass

Rainbow Cafe

P

L'Estaminet

P

Boulevard de Grande Case

Le Petit Hotel

200 ft

100 m

l'Isle Flottante Creperie

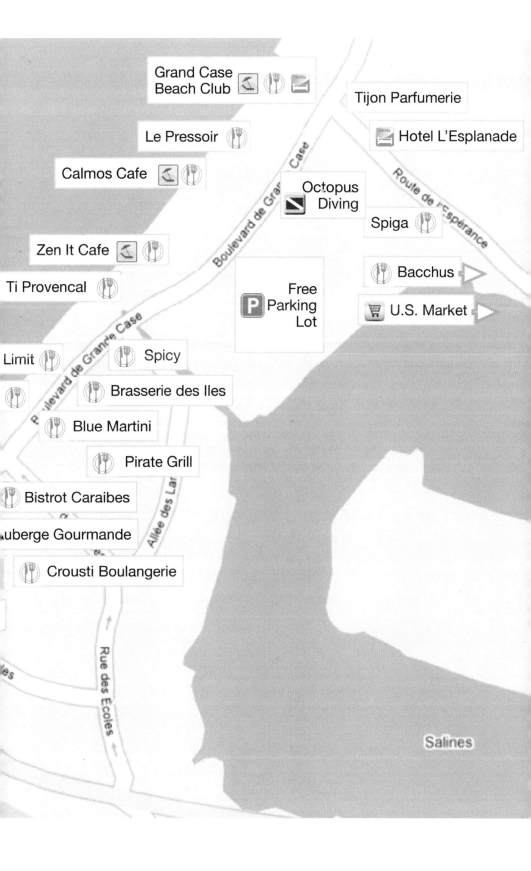

Grand Case Beach Club

Tijon Parfumerie

Le Pressoir

Hotel L'Esplanade

Calmos Cafe

Boulevard de Grande Case

Octopus Diving

Route de l'Espérance

Spiga

Zen It Cafe

Ti Provencal

Free Parking Lot

Bacchus

U.S. Market

Boulevard de Grande Case

Limit

Spicy

Brasserie des Iles

Blue Martini

Pirate Grill

Allée des Lar

Bistrot Caraibes

Auberge Gourmande

Crousti Boulangerie

Rue des Écoles

Salines

Grand Case Directory

It's worth noting that reservations are always a good idea at the gourmet restaurants, especially during high season. Definitely book well in advance for a "Mardi" (Tuesday) when the parade and festivals bring people out in hordes. Your hotel is often willing to call ahead and book for you. Also, if you book in advance, you're more likely to get a great table, especially at those with a beautiful view (hint: they have the even numbered addresses).

During low season, and in general for the casual restaurants, beach bars and lolos, reservations aren't necessarily required, and you can wander by, take a look at the menu, get a feel for the place, and decide for yourself if it's a good fit. The great news about Grand Case is there's always another delicious option!

GOURMET RESTAURANTS	LUCINDA'S RATING	ADDRESS	PHONE
L'Estaminet	★★★★★	139 Blvd. Grand Case	0590 29 00 25
Le Cottage	★★★★★	97 Blvd. Grand Case	0590 29 03 30
L'Auberge Gourmande	★★★★★	89 Blvd. Grand Case	0590 87 73 37
Le Ti Provencal	★★★★☆	48 Blvd. Grand Case	0590 87 05 65
La Villa	★★★★☆	93 Blvd. Grand Case	0590 52 36 59
Le Tastevin	★★★★☆	86 Blvd. Grand Case	0590 87 55 45
Bistrot Caraibes	★★★★☆	81 Blvd. Grand Case	590 29 08 29
Spiga	★★★★☆	Rte. de l'Esperance	0590 52 47 83
L'Escapade	★★★☆☆	94 Blvd. Grand Case	0590 87 75 04
Spicy	★★☆☆☆	17 Blvd. Grand Case	0590 87 07 42
Le Pressoir	★★☆☆☆	30 Blvd. Grand Case	0590 87 76 62
Fishpot	Not Reviewed	82 Blvd. Grand Case	0590 87 50 88
La Marine	Not Reviewed	140 Blvd. Grand Case	0590 87 02 31

CASUAL	RATING	ADDRESS	PHONE
Rainbow Cafe	★★★★☆	176 Blvd. Grand Case	0590 87 55 80
La California	★★★★☆	134 Blvd. Grand Case	0590 87 55 57
Pirate Grill	★★★★☆	Rue de la Republique	0590 83 03 74
Rancho del Sol	★★★★☆	Orient Beach	0590 51 12 12
Piazza Pascal	★★★☆☆	101 Blvd. Grand Case	0590 87 39 21
Brasserie des Iles	★★★☆☆	49 Blvd. Grand Case	0590 87 87 46
Il Nettuno	★★★☆☆	70 Blvd. Grand Case	0590 87 77 38
Le Soleil	★★☆☆☆	60 Blvd. Grand Case	0590 87 92 32
Le Ti Coin Creole	Not Reviewed	Blvd. Grand Case	0590 87 92 09
Blue Martini	Not Reviewed	63 Blvd. Grand Case	0590 29 27 93

BEACH BARS	RATING	ADDRESS	PHONE
Calmos Cafe	★★★★☆	40 Blvd. Grand Case	0590 29 01 85
Zen It	★★★★☆	48 Blvd. Grand Case	0590 87 23 68
Sunset Cafe	★★★☆☆	Petite Plage	0590 29 43 90

LOLOS	RATING	ADDRESS	PHONE
Sky's the Limit	★★★★★	Blvd. Grand Case	0690 35 67 84
Talk of the Town	★★★★☆	Blvd. Grand Case	0590 29 63 89

ETC.	RATING	ADDRESS	PHONE
Hotel L'Esplanade	★★★★★	Rte. de l'Esperance	0590 87 06 55
Octopus Diving	★★★★★	15 Blvd. Grand Case	0590 29 11 27

overview

G rand Case isn't your average whitewashed, Disney-fied destination. It still retains its fishing village roots... plus a glorious collection of 30+ culinary gems. From Gourmet restaurants to Casual bistros, to Beach Bars to the local Lolos... we think you'll find your stomach's delight in Grand Case.

overview

LUCINDA'S LIST
GUIDEBOOK COMPANY

Grand Case
Overall Rating ★★★★★

Why Grand Case? When Steve and I looked to narrow our list of possible tropical destinations in the world, our criteria were simple: warm sun, clear water, pristine sand and a plethora of high-quality restaurants.

No one who knows me is surprised when I say food was a driving factor in selecting Grand Case: typically, I like to plan where I'll be having dinner before I'm even done with lunch. I say I'm "food-dependent," because that's a lot kinder than what many others have called it over the years. But I digress.

Grand Case over-delivered on all counts. Widely considered to be the "**Gourmet Capital of the Caribbean**,"

Grand Case started life as a small fishing village, but now boasts more than 30 phenomenal restaurants. After two trips (one with Steve, aka "Hubby Squirrel," and one with Mom, "Grey Squirrel"), and a total of two months exploring its array of culinary attractions, we still weren't able to see and taste everything on offer in Grand Case... and we were thoroughly convinced its nickname was well earned.

Grand Case is located on the "French side" of St. Martin - yes, the island has two nationalities, French and Dutch, but don't get distracted by that confusing factual tidbit. Grand Case is on the opposite side of the island from busy Dutch St. Marten where you fly into Princess Julianna airport (SXM), and the Dutch capital Philipsburg where all the cruise ships dock, sometimes

five behemoths stacked together at a time. Though it's a short, 20-minute drive, Grand Case couldn't seem further away.

The entire town and its assortment of dining establishments are mostly located on Grand Case Boulevard, the single road (and sometimes single lane) that divides the town between the "haves," i.e. the restaurants on the beach side with glorious sunset water views, and the "have nots," the establishments that work that much harder to achieve culinary excellence. All told, it takes maybe ten minutes to walk the length of Grand Case Boulevard. And yet, on a per-square-foot basis, more culinary goodness is packed into this short walk than I've seen in any neighborhood anywhere else... and I'm spoiled enough to have

lived in New York, San Francisco, Washington and Paris.

It's not just the food that makes Grand Case special. The beach is calm, clean and shockingly empty as most tourists choose to stay in more developed areas. Unlike the famous Orient Beach, packed with pricey beach bars, lounge chairs ten rows deep, obnoxious Jet Skis and hawkers of every variety, the vibe at Grand Case beach is minimalist. On any given day, all you see is a handful of well-loved sailboats dotting the bay, bobbing peacefully in the quiet afternoon breeze. No one disturbs your sun worship.

If you spend enough time in Grand Case, you'll be there for "Mardi," the Tuesday night Harmony parade and celebration held every week during high season. Vendors of jewelry, local art, food, local rums, everything you can imagine, pack themselves on the narrow boulevard. A guy wandering around with a shopping cart full of coconuts will happily cut one open with a machete - right on the spot - for you to enjoy a desert island beverage (a la "Survivor"). The lolos - open-air restaurants - overflow into the street with boisterous patrons gabbing in all manner of indecipherable slang.

If you're imagining a whitewashed, Disney-fied town... don't. This is not a resort. Though its stunning natural scenery provides a perfect Caribbean backdrop, the Boulevard and town itself are more gritty, and, well, real. You shouldn't wander the Boulevard alone in the early hours of the morning. The beach is beautiful and clean, but the street isn't, especially after a brief rainstorm, when you dare not wear that cute little white summer dress.

And yet... Grand Case has one of the most down-to-earth, welcoming cultures you'll ever find, with phenomenal food, wine, rum, beaches, people and hotels. If you want to truly experience the beauty and paradox of the French West Indies, Grand Case is for you.

Restaurant Overview

Grand Case started out life as a modest fishing village, and it's still a modest town, far, far removed from the resorts and cruise ships... except that there are estimated to be 30+ restaurants.

We happily sacrificed ourselves on the altar of butter, creme fraiche and BBQ sauce because, if we don't, who will?

In order to do the food justice across Grand Case, we must first start like the Golden Globe Awards:

Sunset on Grand Case Boulevard

"Fooding Tasting" at Le Cottage

by categorizing. Instead of dramatic film versus comedy (/ musical, how ridiculous is that designation?), we start with the segmentation of Gourmet, Casual, Beach Bar and Lolo. We are in no way suggesting that one category is better than another, or casting aspersions - in fact, some of the best meals we had were also the cheapest. It all depends on your mood, right? In Grand Case, you can find something amazing no matter what you crave.

Gourmet Restaurants... Because Sauciness is Next to Godliness

The true brilliance of Grand Case - and St. Martin overall - is its incredible assortment of gourmet, haute cuisine restaurants. You'll find mostly French (with anywhere from

a small to generous dash of Creole/ island flavor), seafood and Italian cuisines. I was surprised there weren't more sushi restaurants on the island, but apparently the French prefer their seafood cooked, and boy, they do it well, so who can blame them. I joked that I became a shrimpetarian while I was there, and it's not far from the truth. Even though I found out later that the shrimp isn't local, and therefore not exactly fresh... well, I was devastated, but it didn't stop me from loving it. Sauteed in some butter, local spice... mmmm. But you must try the local seafood, it's amazing. The grouper, trigger fish, trunk fish.. and lobster, oh my! I also rediscovered my addiction to foie gras and duck. No one else does foie gras the way the French do.

Foie Gras at L'Estaminet

But at the end of the day... it's the sauces that keep you salivating and coming back for more. Every one of the gourmet restaurants specializes in some sort of saucy scintillation. Whether you order the fish, shrimp, duck, or filet... there's always some cosmically rich, flavorful sauce to go along with it. And the beauty of truly great sauce is that it satisfies a craving you didn't even know you had, and you don't need to eat as much to feel satisfied. Portions are more European-sized, not super-sized, which leaves you free to

Chocolate fondue cake at La Villa

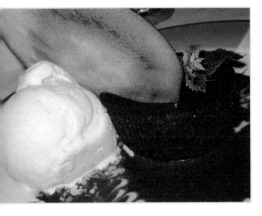

experiment with more delectable courses.

Oh, and did I mention the wine lists? For the oenophiles out there, you will in no way be disappointed. Unless you're a California wine snob - there's not a whole lot of new world wines. But who cares? The French wine selection is as good as I've seen in many Parisian restaurants, and the sommeliers extremely knowledgeable. I've been a huge fan of Chateauneuf du Pape for twenty years, and Sancerre, and Cotes du Rhones... but while we were there I became well acquainted with my new friend Chateau Margaux. Every restaurant had a vast selection of French wines, many of them surprisingly reasonable. Of course, St. Martin is technically part of France, so no surprise they have the inside track on the good stuff.

But wait, I've left out the best part: DESSERT. I've never eaten so much dessert in my life - or at least not since I embraced Weight Watchers two years ago - and OMG, it was spectacular. My husband claims to not have a sweet tooth, but we just couldn't hold ourselves back. Most every restaurant trots out their version of chocolate lava cake with vanilla ice cream, and wow it is all good. That said, I'm pretty sure my all-time favorite desserts were the souffles at Le Cottage. Incredible.

Oh wait, there's still more! Each and every restaurant on the Boulevard prides itself on having a special homemade digestif that they bring to your table at the end of the meal. Most are flavored rums, some brandy-based, some who-knows-what... but all provide a perfect conclusion to a fantastic meal.

L'Estaminet is definitely one of our top picks - even though it's on the non-scenic side of the Boulevard, they make up for it with their exquisite culinary concoctions. The filet layered with goat cheese and truffle remoulade was luxurious, while their signature four-tiered rum digestif knocked me over.

Le Cottage is over-the-top in their creativity and presentation, and it works. You won't always recognize your meal, but go with it, and you'll be thrilled. I've rarely seen that level of innovation at a restaurant; it was reminiscent of places like Cyrus in Healdsburg.

Meet the Owners

These are small, intimate restaurants, and more often than not, labors of love as the owners are cooking, hosting and/or waiting on you. Be nice to them, and they'll be nice to you!

L'Auberge Gourmande's sauces made my head spin, as did their seared foie gras. Le Ti Provencal blew my mother and me away with the simplicity and perfection of local seafood preparation. The warm trunk fish salad... magnifique!

GOURMET RESTAURANTS	LUCINDA'S RATING
L'Estaminet	★★★★★
Le Cottage	★★★★★
L'Auberge Gourmande	★★★★★
Le Ti Provencal	★★★★☆
La Villa	★★★★☆
Le Tastevin	★★★★☆
Bistrot Caraibes	★★★★☆
Spiga	★★★★☆
L'Escapade	★★★☆☆
Spicy	★★☆☆☆
Le Pressoir	★★☆☆☆
Fishpot	Not Reviewed
La Marine	Not Reviewed

Pirate Grill

La Villa may win the prize for the best chocolate lava cake, though Bistrot Caraibes is a close second with their unexpected "Pop Rocks."

But these few favorites are by no means the end of the road for Grand Case. The culinary delights of this town overfloweth.

Casual Restaurants... For Those Quieter Nights

Entrecote at Rainbow Cafe

In between the outdoor lolos and the high-end, pricey gourmet restaurants, complete with $500 bottles of wine if you choose to go crazy, you can still find a good, solid, casual meal in Grand Case. It will likely entail a perfectly crispy thin-crust pizza, or pasta with cream sauce, or your basic steak frites... and there's absolutely nothing wrong with any of it.

Though I put it in the casual category mostly because it isn't open for dinner, and it's more of a wine store, the food at Bacchus is most certainly not second rate. We had a phenomenal lunch there: duck breast layered over bacon layered over cream and butter, layered over sliced potatoes, all in a tasty island sauce. I could feel my arteries clogging with every bite, and still I pushed on, deciding it was worth it to lose a couple days off my life. And did I mention it's an incredible wine store as well? Go there even if it's just to pick up a bottle or two for later. They also have packaged gourmet foods, perfect for a beach picnic.

Recently reopened under new ownership, **Rainbow Cafe** is the perfect spot for a delicious steak or burger. Their "nems" appetizer was particularly tasty, but perhaps I'm just a sucker for golden fried Vietnamese spring rolls. Right on the beach, it also provides modernist beach chairs and umbrellas, so it's almost a beach bar... except that their food is a cut above your average beach restaurant.

If the purpose of your outing is to find the best of the thin-crust pizzas, look no further than **La California**. They have an extensive list of options, and they don't disappoint. Beyond their pizza, they're also considered the best moules frites (mussels & french fries) on the Boulevard, and for good reason. They offer 15 different preparations,

Sunset Tip

La California and Rainbow Cafe are two of the best casual restaurants for watching the sunset with an aperitif.

from traditional Provencal to crazy concoctions. I must have gone through an entire baguette soaking up the delectable sauce before I reined myself in... though it might have been more like Steve had to physically restrain me before I lifted the bowl and tilted my head back... but who's keeping track?

In the unexpectedly delicious camp, the **Pirate Grill** is a unique destination, full of pirate kitsch and an X-rated bathroom. But the food! Imagine a bachelor living alone on a boat, and what would he cook?

CASUAL RESTAURANTS	LUCINDA'S RATING
Rainbow Cafe	★★★★☆
La California	★★★★☆
Pirate Grill	★★★★☆
Rancho del Sol	★★★★☆
Piazza Pascal	★★★☆☆
Brasserie des Iles	★★★☆☆
Il Nettuno	★★★☆☆
Le Soleil	★★☆☆☆
Le Ti Coin Creole	Not Reviewed
Blue Martini	Not Reviewed

Grilled meats and seafood, of course! With baked potatoes slathered in creme fraiche. Surprisingly hearty fare.

One of our favorite go-to casual restaurants when we are feeling over-gourmeted (or hungover) is **Brasserie des Iles**. It's a quiet, open restaurant on the "wrong" side of the Grand Case Boulevard, so no beautiful views. What it does have is traditional, authentic French pizzas. If you've never had one, try one - and don't plan to share. It's such a delectable thin-crust that you will easily inhale the entire thing. Try spritzing on a little of the spicy oil. Trust me.

Brasserie des Iles also serves proper ice cream, both in the dining room and on the street. Delicious on a warm Caribbean evening. They have decent salads - and greens are in surprisingly short supply for a tropical island. All told, nothing exciting, just solid, reasonable fare. Though, I will say that we often ran into the local gendarmes eating there. Perhaps that is why it is so mellow and quiet?

But wait... don't feel like leaving your hotel at all? Then it must be a night for **Rancho Del Sol**. They DELIVER. Yes, deliver. "Livraison." A magical French word for those nights when you feel like a crispy critter because you underestimated the strength of the Caribbean sun, and overestimated your natural "base" tan and decided to go with SPF 8. Their pizzas are also phenomenal, even after a trip over the hill from Orient Beach, and their extensive menu means everyone can find their comfort food.

If you're craving some good ol' Italian carbs, **Piazza Pascal** is the place to go. You might be tempted by Il Nettuno's seaside views, but Piazza Pascal definitely wins on the satisfying pasta front.

Beach Bars... Lounging the Day Away (& Night!)

Though most people don't think of Grand Case as a beach, the entire Boulevard hugs a mile long bay, complete with a pristine, white sand beach. Being on the western side of the island, Grand Case beach is protected from the surf you sometimes find on the Atlantic, windward side. There aren't really noticeable differences between high/low tides (unless a swell is coming in, i.e. a storm, in which case all bets are off). The beach isn't always that wide - some areas are but a slim strip between a retaining wall and the waves.

Zen It Cafe

BEACH BARS	LUCINDA'S RATING
Calmos Cafe	★★★★☆
Zen It	★★★★☆
Sunset Cafe	★★★☆☆

OK, so first let's admit this isn't Orient Beach, chock-full of beach bar options where you can't pitch a beach towel without someone charging you $10. There aren't that many beach bars, probably because most of the beachfront locations are taken up by the amazing gourmet restaurants (if you're confused by that statement, revisit the gourmet section above).

And yet... it's this complete lack of attention as a beach destination that makes Grand Case the perfect place to lounge at a beach bar.

Of the beach bars, by far our favorite - probably in all of St. Martin - is **Calmos Cafe**. We first stumbled on Calmos Cafe by accident - you can't see if from the street, only from the beach - as we headed down the dark alleyway one night

Sunset Cafe

intent on a rum punch before turning in for the evening. What luck. You get to the cafe and find a full open-air bar, complete with picnic tables and, wait for it, beach chairs perfectly situated at the edge of where the waves gently nip at your toes. That night we left after just one drink at the bar (during which the bar started spitting on me - turns out that's a "service" by which it douses you in pesticide, a service I have since come to appreciate), but we vowed to return the next night when we saw the cheeseburgers float by on a tray. Over the course of our two months, we spent many an enjoyable day and evening at Calmos, and sometimes well into the wee hours. It's a great place to party with friends or just have a simple meal on the beach.

On the days and nights when Calmos gets too busy, or if you're looking for the best full breakfast in Grand Case (high season only), go two doors down to **Zen It Cafe**. With the same French owner, Zen It is a simplified, toned-down version of Calmos. Fewer beach chairs means it's quieter during the day. They serve a solid breakfast, with the best French cafe au lait on the Boulevard, and more importantly, they serve it until 11:30 a.m., a real bonus if you're on true island vacation schedule. They also offer WiFi (pronounced Wee-fee by the

Calmos Cafe

French), though it's sometimes sporadic. In the evenings, it's a nice quiet place to dip your toes in the water by moon and candlelight, while sipping on a delightful mojito.

Further north on the beach, past the end of Grand Case Boulevard and into Grand Case Beach Club, you'll find **Sunset Cafe**. The cafe itself is not technically on the sand, but it is right above the Beach Club's private beach. Well, it's not really

Beach Tip

You have to pay to lounge at Grand Case Beach Club. If you eat at Calmos or Zen It, you get comfortable chairs and

private - anyone can go there, but you have to ask to be let in at the gate. I believe you can order from the Sunset Cafe to be brought down to you on the beach. Food at the Sunset Cafe is respectable, though nothing earth-shattering. Really you're there because of the location and beautiful views. One bonus - they serve breakfast, all too rare in these parts, though only until 10:30.

Beyond these three, there is Captain Frenchy's and Love Hotel at the other end of the Boulevard, but we never basked there. If you're looking for a plethora of beach bars, or a big beach party atmosphere, head to Orient Beach.

Sky's the Limit

Lolos... Hello-lo Tasty Grilled Goodness!

I'm not entirely sure what "lolos" stands for, but it must in some way mean "local," because that's the best place to start. You will find lolos all over the island - the level of sophistication is akin to a taco truck, but instead with a **50-gallon drum** cut in half to create a barbeque. They are run by island locals who have clearly spent generations perfecting their spicy cuisine. In the heart of Grand Case, you will find four lolos (or five, hard to tell), all grouped together, their picnic tables running into one another. You can smell them from a block away, the cloud of barbeque aroma billowing in all directions, and you find yourself, willingly or not, like Toucan Sam, following your nose (it always knows!).

We weren't at the lolos every day of our first six-week visit... but let's just say that if they had a loyalty club, we would have maxed our cards and gotten a freebie more than once. Start with the fact that a beer is $1. Need I say more? Still not convinced? OK, they do a 1:1 conversion from euro to dollars (most only take cash). And they're cheap. But is the food any good? Umm, YEAH. The ribs (travers de

"Rib Food"

porc) practically fall off the bone when you pick them up. They are the greasiest, most succulent morsels ever. When you first see the bottle of "Kraft" barbeque sauce in the basket on the table, you're worried, until you realize that the bottle is ancient, and was clearly repurposed from its original generic contents long ago to instead hold the keys to the kingdom of tastiness. It would seem that each lolo has its own basket assortment of condiments, with their special spices and sauces.

Beyond the ribs, the "shrimp food" (Crevettes Creole) are perfectly light and juicy, in a tasty Creole sauce that as far as I can tell involves butter, garlic, onions and local crack. For some reason this dish is always served with potato salad, which is unexpectedly, crazy good, with peas and carrots (note: the secret to this dish might have been in the vat of "extra heavy" mayonnaise I glimpsed in the kitchen). You should also get the local red rice and beans, perfect to absorb the tasty saucy goodness (and a dash of Matouk's hot sauce, for the bold), plus a nice dollop of cole slaw, the likes of which I've never found in health-conscious California. And like ordering a Diet Coke with your Big Mac, you get a tiny "green salad" comprised of one piece of lettuce and one shred of carrot, hanging onto the edge of the plate for dear life. What is funny

Talk of the Town

is that you will also sometimes receive spaghetti, and maybe even macaroni and cheese. The combination sounds downright odd, until you taste it all together. Your plate bulges... as will your waistline if you're not careful. This is not a dieter-friendly stretch of sand.

LOLOS	LUCINDA'S RATING
Sky's the Limit	★★★★★
Talk of the Town	★★★★☆

The best part? **Each of these dishes was roughly $10.** Everything there is ridiculously cheap... with one notable exception. One night our dinner companion attempted to order the grilled lobster, and was told the last one remaining was so large it was $80, and no they don't do half-lobsters. We saw them grilling the lobsters - basted with gallons of butter dripping into the fire - and were not surprised people were willing to shell out for them. Just be sure to ask the price when you order, as the lobster aren't in line with the other items.

About halfway through our stay, we learned that of the seemingly similar lolos clustered together, the locals only eat at **"Sky's the Limit."** We became loyal followers after our first visit. It's the one with the blue picnic tables... and $1 beers (some lolos charge a downright usurious $1.50), and the extra spaghetti and macaroni. Order the "shrimp food" or "rib food."

There are a few other lolos and lolo-like restaurants we missed: Au Coin Des Amis and La Bodega, plus Captain Frenchy's at the end of the Boulevard next to a pink Creole-style place (no one seems to know the name of it). For the first two, we skipped them because frankly no one recommended them the way they did Sky's the Limit and Talk of the Town, and, well, we were addicted, what can I say? All of these lolos are targets for our next visit.

If I Only Had One Meal in Grand Case...

The whole point of this Grand Case Overview is to help you understand why it's worth spending weeks, months, or the rest of your life in Grand Case... I mean, I'm convinced. Now I just need to convince my husband, right? But I recognize not everyone has the luxury of an extended visit.

So... if I only had one meal in Grand Case... what would I do?

As usual, the answer comes down to mood. It all depends, right? So, here is a quick summary of my various favorites, in order of overall preference:

- **L'Estaminet** - best gourmet cuisine overall
- **Le Cottage** - best innovation and food presentation
- **Sky's the Limit** - best lolo
- **Calmos Cafe** - best beach bar (and rum, and burger, and party spot)
- **Bacchus** - best wine store and gourmet lunch
- **La California** - best mussels/frites and thin-crust pizzas
- **Bistrot Caraibes** - best lobster
- **Zen It** - best breakfast and beach lounging
- **Rancho Del Sol** - best delivery

Bottom Line

It doesn't take much to have a wonderful time in French St. Martin. This is no third-world country... it's a little slice of all that is good and wonderful about France, in a tropical paradise.

With amazing cuisine and gorgeous scenery, Grand Case is the best of the best, with 30+ independent and innovative restaurants packed cheek by jowl along a one-lane boulevard. With such intense competition, you can find dizzyingly satisfying cuisine for every budget and mood. Don't miss out on your next trip!

MOULIN A SEL

travel tips

*W*hen you're traveling, you want to make sure you know the lay of the land - literally. We've put together a quick cheat sheet of helpful tips to make your trip to the French side of St. Martin as enjoyable and stress-free as possible.

LUCINDA'S LIST
GUIDEBOOK COMPANY

Travel Tips

As much as we like to believe food is the only thing that really matters when we travel, with maybe a few beaches and beach bars sprinkled in, we admit there are sometimes other considerations. We've compiled a quick list of those tidbits of advice and information that we thought would be most conducive to an enjoyable trip to Grand Case, and generally St. Martin.

Show Me the Money

The French side of St. Martin is always priced in euros, but **everyone accepts dollars** as well. The trick is what's the conversion? Some restaurants offer a 1 euro = 1 dollar conversion rate if you pay cash - do it, it's worth it. Other restaurants will give you an overall rate, like 1 euro = 1.2 dollars, and will compute the bill for you in both currencies. But if you plan to use your credit card, most restaurants will put it through in euros, which means you'll have to pay whatever usurious exchange rate your bank has decided on that day. Bottom line? Pay cash if you can.

But how do you get cash? This is another trick to know. **None of the ATMs on the French side dispense U.S. Dollars**. Only euros. For that matter, ATMs aren't that common on the French side. Grand Case Boulevard doesn't have ANY, so don't plan to pick up some euros when you get there (the closest one is outside town, at either the pharmacy or the post office). If you need U.S. Dollars, which are definitely the better deal if you're eating at the lolos or other 1:1 establishments, then you need to head to the Dutch side. There is a bank as soon as you cross the border, a few minutes past Marigot, and just after the Princess casino. This is your closest source of U.S. Dollars to Grand Case. It's only about a 10-15 minute drive usually, and happens to be located next to the cheaper Dutch grocery store, so try to bundle your trip.

Parlez Vous Francais?

French St. Martin is just that - French. It's actually a "collectivite," which is considered to be part of France, similar to how Hawaii is part of the U.S. (as opposed to Guam). Schools teach children in French. Prices are required to be in euros. The list goes on. You will definitely know that you're not in the United States anymore.

Closest U.S. Dollars to Grand Case

But language? That's the good news. Roughly **99% of the people we encountered there spoke English**, and spoke it very well at that. Not everyone can have an existential conversation in English, but that's what your friends and spouse are for, right? The good news is you will have absolutely no problem getting around with English. There were only two times in six weeks that my husband required me to come to his rescue with my rusty French: when he was trying to explain to the France Telecom salesperson how he dropped his iPhone and cracked the screen and wanted it replaced (that will be $200, please, doh!); and when he needed a replacement screw for his sunglasses. In both cases, Steve's rudimentary French was in trouble (I called his particular dialect "St-ench"), but it was extremely rare. Don't be scared off if you don't speak French. You'll get by just fine.

On the other hand, if you're like me and want to brush off that college semester you spent in Grenoble, France, well then you're in luck. Though the island locals tend to prefer English (probably because they were forced to speak French in school), the many French transplants who own and work in many of the restaurants and shops **LOVE when you speak French.** Well, they do as long as you have a decent accent that doesn't cause their ears to bleed. So just like when I was studying in France, it took a couple weeks before they would reply in French, but once I had re-found my accent, it was great. They were thrilled to converse with me in French, and help further my understanding. Sadly, my accent seemed to imply a more extensive vocabulary than I had retained in the past two decades, so I often had no idea what they were actually saying... but it was all good. Smiling helps.

What to Wear? (Or Not)

Many of the gourmet restaurants on the French side are just as chi-chi as you'd find in New York or Paris. Their prices aren't that different, and the quality of food is right up there. And, you're in France, right? So if you want to, you can get dressed up for dinner. But here's the thing. You're on a Caribbean island. The waiters at the beach bars don't wear shoes... nor sometimes shirts, for that matter. Even if you're going to one of the nicest restaurants in town, both men and women could get away with nice shorts, nice top and sandals. There is no shirt/tie dress code here. So, **there is a wide spectrum of what is acceptable**, but I certainly wouldn't show up at a nice restaurant in cut-offs and t-shirt.

In general, in the evenings you will mostly see "resort casual" - strappy dresses with sandals, white pants, khaki shorts, the usual suspects that you'd see in a beach town. Some do dress to the nines, and there's nothing wrong with that, and no one will look askance at you - so if you've been waiting for an excuse to wear that fun strapless dress with slingback metallic heels, don't hesitate.

If you're planning to head to the casinos or nightclubs on the Dutch side, you might even want to pull out your Miami party outfit. But Grand Case is a bit more laid-back.

Digestif at Rainbow Cafe

Don't Get Bit

Two items you should NEVER go without? sunscreen and bug repellent. The sun is hot (duh) and the bugs are ravenous, especially at dusk. On occasion, they have outbreaks of Dengue Fever, a particularly nasty virus transmitted by mosquitos, so **do NOT play Russian roulette with these bugs**. They are not your tame domestic U.S. variety - these guys play for keeps. I highly recommend investing in the Belgian bug repellant sold on the island in most pharmacies and grocery stores, and even some hotels: JAICO Mosquito Milk Repellent, "Tropical Version." It's a recognizable white bottle with a green top, and even smells better than your average repellant. Luckily many restaurants and bars will also share their supply if you forget and go out naked.

Channeling Miss Manners

St. Martin bills itself as "the friendly island," and I certainly found that to be true. It is also a French island, meaning **they observe French niceties and etiquette** that Americans may not be used to. When you enter a store or restaurant, or anywhere for that matter, it's considered rude not to say hello and acknowledge the person working there. If you went into a person's house, you wouldn't ignore them, would you? It's the same idea. Even if it's a mangled "bonjour" or "Salut," it will be greatly appreciated and go a long way to ensuring you have an enjoyable experience.

During the day, the island is very, very casual. It's quite common to see people barefoot wandering through towns like Grand Case, or eating at the casual beach bars or lolos in their bathing suits with just a see-through cover up or pareo (wrap). That said, Marigot is more of a town - you want to wear proper shoes and clothing. On the beach itself... well, on the French beaches you'll sometimes see topless sunbathers, though that depends on the beach. At Orient Beach (where Club "O" is famous as a naturalist haven, i.e. the Full Monty) you'll see the most toplessness. Speedos? I saw a few, but I wouldn't recommend it unless you are actually European and can pull it off. But please, whatever you do, don't wear socks with your sandals. It's never cold enough to require socks. Don't waste your suitcase space!

In Grand Case especially, the restaurants are very small, and you'll often find that the person who showed you to your table, and then took your order is, in fact, one of the owners. Talk to them. They are lovely people who care deeply about their restaurant, and can be very helpful and even friendly. We met wonderful people in our time there. Many of them love to meet new people and be engaged in conversation, and let me tell you, they will often give you the best local advice... not to mention extra drinks at the end of the evening. If you get really friendly, don't be freaked out when at the end of the evening they give the "bissou," This isn't as scary as it sounds! It's the French practice of lightly kissing you on first the left, then the right cheek, and they're in no way trying to get cheeky.

Last, but very important, if you toast with someone, say for example the waiter who has brought you the traditional end of the evening digestif of delicious rum and you wisely invite them to join you in a toast, **LOOK THEM IN THE EYE**. It is not only considered rude not to, but there is a saying that you will have seven years of bad... ahem... let's just say I strongly recommend not running afoul of this curse!

It's a Dangerous World

In the eight weeks that we stayed in Grand Case, we never personally felt threatened or in any way unsafe. We often stayed out past midnight. As one local explained it, the majority of crime in St. Martin isn't violent - it's more a matter of someone relieving you of your "worldly burdens"... like cameras, wallets, etc.

All that said, we strongly advise you to use good sense. Especially during low season, when there aren't as many people out and about, don't walk home late at night, and definitely not alone. Three of our friends were held up at knife point, walking home at 3 a.m., resulting in the loss of some money; luckily no one was hurt. Police were called, and the perpetrators were in fact apprehended 20 minutes later. I certainly wouldn't say Grand Case is a hotbed of crime, but it never, ever hurts to play it safe. **If it's after 11 p.m., don't wander around alone** - especially if you are a woman. And definitely keep your eyes open, even if you're in a group. Don't leave your stuff unattended on the beach during the day, or "locked" in your car.

Walking seems like such a straightforward option, but that assumes paved sidewalks and wide boulevards, neither of which are to be found in Grand Case. Drivers are amazingly courteous, but remember that you are pretty much walking in the main thoroughfares and must share the space with other pedestrians, motorbikes, cars, tour buses, and vehicles of every stripe. Wheelchairs would be insane.

To Tip or Not To Tip?

I think it was week four or so before I finally felt like I had decoded the complex tipping protocols. If you've ever been to France, you know there is a magic phrase "service est compris." Service is included. In France, waiters are looked on more as professionals, and they are salaried along those lines. The restaurant already includes service charges when they price their menu items, or else adds the service charge, so you don't have to. Of course, anti-socialists would point

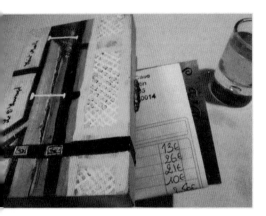

"L'Addition" at Le Ti Provencal

out this takes away your freedom to express displeasure and therefore the waiters have no incentive to be good... which is a fair point. But overall, we had good experiences, especially at the nicer restaurants and when we were friendly. If you feel that a waiter has particularly outdone himself, you leave at most a couple euro coins after you sign the bill. There is no line on the charge slip for tip. Such a simple world.

And yet, somehow, it is more complicated in St. Martin. Sometimes there was a line for tip on the charge slip. Do you use it? Unclear. In that case, it makes sense to ask if a service charge was included. But be very careful. Don't ask if a "tip" was included, because in their world, these are two different things - a tip is the extra coins, not the service. So if you ask them if a "tip" was included, they will often say "no"... and you will leave an American tip, which is way more than appropriate (yes, I fell for that one a couple times).

Beyond restaurant tipping, hotels will usually also include service charges so you don't need to worry about it, but be sure to ask. It's always good to leave a few dollars for the housekeepers. And always tip your taxi driver a couple dollars - we were surprised to find how often we ended up with the same driver. It's a small island.

Rental Cars

During our first six-week trip, we started out by renting a car for the first week. We knew we'd want to do a lot of exploring, and had no idea how easy it would be to get around. Luckily, our hotel offered us an introduction to a local car rental place called Justice (http://www.justicecarrental.com/). Renting for a week, we not only got great rates and a free day, they picked us up from the airport, a major bonus when you have no idea how to get from SXM to the French side.

After a week, we gave up the car when we realized we rarely felt a need to leave Grand Case. Then after a week without a car, we rented one for the rest of our trip because, well, mostly because we wanted to be able to buy groceries... and get to the Bacchus wine store! But also because we realized the best beaches - Friar's Bay, Orient Beach, etc - simply aren't on the main road where the buses stop.

My advice? Rent a car. But before you pony up for a name-brand rental company, ask your hotel who they recommend. More often than not, they can help you find a reputable local rental agency. Just keep in mind this is not going to be one of those brand-new huge sedans you get in the U.S. - most have been on the island longer than the French. For that matter, I recommend getting the absolute smallest car you can handle, not only because it is cheaper, but because it will be far, far easier to park and navigate those incredibly narrow city streets.

Free Parking

Parking in Grand Case... well, luckily we didn't have to do it very often since we were walking distance. So my first recommendation is to actually stay in Grand Case.

That said, coming from California where I always pay for parking, even in front of my own house (you have to pay for a permit), I was pleasantly surprised to see that parking meters do not exist in St. Martin in general. Now, that doesn't mean parking is easy. With an incredibly narrow main boulevard in Grand Case, you are hard-pressed to find street parking on a crowded evening, but **there is a handy parking lot just downtown** next to the Cultural Center. It's free. Even if an old guy walks up and asks for $4, ignore him; it's free. There's another lot at the other end of town and I think they charge $5 in the evenings, but some restaurants will credit you on your bill.

Special note: Tuesdays in high season... when the Mardi festival was going on (every Tuesday, January - April), that was definitely the exception to easy parking. Parking on Mardi was a bit of a nightmare from what we observed from the restaurant patios, sipping our aperitif. The good news is the

Parking Lot in Grand Case

locals tend to open up their front lawns and charge you a couple euros for the privilege. There is also street parking, but it is very tight, and get used to parallel parking right up against a stone wall. If you're headed to Mardi, I'd recommend calling a taxi.

In Marigot, we often found parking downtown near the market, but we always felt lucky when we did.

Taxi!

We found taxis to be fairly reliable in St. Martin. You can call the dispatch anywhere from the French side: **0590 87 56 54**. In Marigot there are taxi stands, but I don't think there is one in Grand Case, and you can't usually just walk out and flag one down; that's not how it works. Just have your restaurant call for a taxi for you. Keep in mind there are various surcharges: $4 for an extra passenger, $1 per luggage (though this may vary), 25% if it's after 10 p.m., 50% if it's after midnight and before 6 a.m.. You should tip your driver: standard rate is ~ 15%.

Buses... Only for the Intrepid

Had we still been in our 20's and feeling cash-strapped, we would have attempted the bus system. It seemed fairly simple: at random intervals, a vehicle would arrive in a general vicinity, with a sign that indicated the direction and general end point of the route. Foolproof, right? Especially when the vehicle could be anything from an actual bus to a dilapidated VW van from the 70's, with or without air conditioning, chock-full of strangers, with a roughly 80% chance of making its final destination. I can't imagine why, but Steve was never up for the adventure... and I admit, I didn't push very hard. That said, it **costs between $1 or $1.50** depending on the quality of the vehicle, so if you're on a budget, nothing wrong with it, especially if you're going to a major destination like Marigot or Grand Case.

What If It's An Emergency?

I'm exceedingly thankful that we didn't have any emergencies during our time in St. Martin, medical or otherwise. If you find yourself in trouble, on the **Dutch side you can call 911**. On the **French side, dial direct:**

- **St. Martin Ambulance**: 15 or 590-87-86-25

- **St. Martin Police/Emergency**: 17 or 590-87-88-33

If it's not an emergency, I would start by calling the front desk at your hotel. You can try simply visiting one of the Doctors on the island, or check first with the pharmacies - they sometimes have a Dr. who has office hours.

Assortment of other Random Tidbits

- **Electricity** - Yep, you guessed it: European electricity, 220 voltage. You will want to bring a transformer and/or converter for your items. Many hotels have transformers they will loan you for your stay - ask in advance, and it will save you $$ and luggage space. Note to self: just getting a converter isn't always sufficient! Appliances will need a transformer, a much more involved item than the plug converter. For your computer, you'll probably need a special converter - check with your manufacturer. Trust me. You don't want to fry your electronics.

- **Time Zone** - St. Martin follows Atlantic Standard Time (AST). That means during the summer, when the East Coast is on daylight savings time, St. Martin is the same as the East Coast. During the winter, St. Martin is one hour ahead of the East Coast.

- **"Island Time"** - Many shops on the French side close down during noon to 2 p.m., as is traditional in France when shopkeepers take their lunch.

Restaurants often close in between lunch and dinner, and don't start dinner service until 6 p.m. During low season... well, it all kind of depends on the day. For that matter, 1 p.m. doesn't necessarily mean 1 p.m. exactly. "Island time" means everyone moves to the beat of his/her own drum, not necessarily the tick of the clock. If it's really going to ruin your day, the trick is to call ahead to check if they're open.

- **Visas & Passports** - Yes, you need a valid U.S. passport to enter St. Martin (and get back into the States, for that matter!). You don't need a visa unless you plan to stay for longer than 90 days (lucky dog!). In that case, you need to contact the French consulate to apply for a visa. You can get a one-year visa if you don't plan to work (or at least don't plan to get paid to work), and can prove that you have sufficient means to not be a burden on the system, including your own health insurance.

- **Weather** - Weather in St. Martin seems to generally be in the 80's all year round. The trick is how often it rains - seldom during high season, more often during low, and frequently when you hit prime hurricane season (July - October).

- **Airport** - Even though you're going to French St. Martin, you won't be flying into the local Grand Case airport, L'Esperance. Princess Juliana Airport (SXM) on the Dutch side is a major airport that can accommodate large jumbo jets flying direct from major cities like NY and Paris.

- **Phones** - To call French St. Martin from another the U.S., start by dialing 011, then 590 590 (yes, it's repeated twice), followed by a local six digit number. On the island, you'll dial 00 before the 590-590. If you're calling the Dutch side from off island, you'll want to dial 011-599-54, plus a five digit local number.

- **Driving under the influence** - Be aware that France enforces their drunk driving laws, and they are stricter: the limit in St. Martin is 0.05 BAC versus 0.08 in the U.S. For a 150 lb man, one drink will raise his BAC by 0.02.

Bottom Line

The French side of St. Martin is different enough from the U.S. to feel like another country, but not so much so that you shouldn't enjoy the differences. Keep in mind these simple travel tips and you'll have no problems.

On the Dutch side, you'll find things are more similar to the U.S. - same electricity, easy to get U.S. Dollars, everyone speaks English, same 911 in an emergency.

Whichever side of the island you choose to stay on, St. Martin is so tourist-friendly, you won't have any major issues. And when in doubt, ask a local...

Fan Favorites - Travel Tips

Our Facebook fans have plenty of additional tips to help make your trip a success:

 Tyrinda - if you buy a calling card make sure to get it from there because the ones from the US won't work. Also monitor you account because the banking system is different and when you use your card they sometimes put extra holds on your card. And what every you do don't make calls from the hotel I learned the hard way. One call cost me over $150 I saw it on my account when I got home.

 Liana - If you go to one of the jewelry stores on the dutch side they let you use their phone for free, to call Canada or the States, Its called the Riviera, the people in their are great and so were their prices on gold!!

 Kristin - 2 things, a Capital One credit card has no foreign transaction fees and if you are a Bank of America customer, you can use your B of A ATM card here at our Scotia banks and as they are "sister banks" there are no ATM fees whatsoever.

 Elizabeth - Buses and taxies go everywhere and aren't expensive. English is fine on both sides. Dollars. Locate groceries, they aren't everywhere. U can buy good wine at any convenience store, grocery, even jewelry stores in town. It's impossible to find a bad meal. Food is wonderful on both sides. Beaches are beautiful. People friendly, particularly on Dutch side. Love the casinos. Have fun.

 Bonnie - You have to go to the "rum" store for the chocolate and banana and other flavoured rums--yum!! Its in the section of stores where the cruise ships dock. Go to the Ralph Lauren store and directly across the street from it is a sort of 'ally' with a few more shops- its on the left side.

Fan Favorites - Travel Tips

 Juanita - Gas on the French side seems to be better regulated and cheaper!

 Dianne - Yes rent a car about 200 for the week less expensive then taking cabs and if you stay out late and planning to spend time all over the island a car is your best bet.... Dollar Rent a Car right across the street from the airport..they built a new grocery store by the Pelican it is very good and a there is a great small grocery store across the street from the Royal Islander Club La Plage no need to speak french or convert american dollars

 Pat - Don't forget Mr Tablecloth or Belgian Chocolate Box in St. Philipsburg

 Jean-Philippe - having been on both side of the island I can attest that the markets the Dutch side are cheaper, but on the french side, the choice is better and meat and vegetables are certainly of better quality. US Market in Grand-Case and in Marigot are my best bet.

 Melinda - To check out the local St. Martin weather: http://www.wunderground.com/tropical or http://www.nhc.noaa.gov.

 Wendy - My favorite part of St. Marten was sailing on the America Cup Boats...Very inexpensive and a lot of fun:) If you race in the bay where the cruise ships come in and then the Rum Regatta follows..great day:)

 Mollie - Just got back yesterday, if you are staying on French side take the time to go to the new area Porto Cupecoy and shop at Le Gourmet grocery. So much cheaper! Also inside the casino close to Cupecoy beach is an Italian restaurant called la Gondola, eat there. Best Italian ever!

gourmet restaurant reviews

Gourmet restaurants are a dime a dozen in Grand Case - you can't sneeze without stumbling into one. I suspect it's this close competition that drives the chefs to create some of the tastiest, most innovative French cuisine available outside Paris.

gourmet restaurants

LUCINDA'S LIST
GUIDEBOOK COMPANY

Just the Facts

Price Level:
$$$$

Category:
French

Meals Served:
Dinner

Location:
139 Grand
Case Boulevard

Phone:
0590 29 00 25

Credit Cards:
Visa

Website:
NA

Currency:
10% better than
market

*Outdoor
seating:*
None

Parking:
Nearby lot

Good for:
Foodies, Groups

Pros

Delicious and innovative food,
perfectly prepared and
presented
Warm, solicitous service; Intimate,
beautifully appointed
atmosphere, even without views

Cons

No views or outdoor seating

L'Estaminet
Overall Rating ★★★★★

The first time we went to dinner at
L'Estaminet was during high season
with several friends, all residents of
St. Martin. It had recently captured
the #1 rating on Trip Advisor for
restaurants in St. Martin, and we
were all looking forward to trying it.
It did not disappoint. It was
delicious food and great fun,
though in the end we were so
raucous I'm impressed they didn't
throw us out.

When I returned to Grand Case
during "quiet" season (August) with
my mom, I knew we had to go
back to L'Estaminet. It was my
favorite meal from the six weeks we
had previously spent there, and I
wanted to go back. But, wisely, I
knew we couldn't go early in the
trip or the temptation to return
again and again would be too
great to withstand, and our
"research" trip would be a disaster.
I was wise to wait. It is without a
doubt my favorite restaurant on

Grand Case Boulevard... and definitely in my top five in the world.

Food at L'Estaminet

On our first visit, I had the gazpacho as an appetizer, mostly because I wanted the duck for my main course, and the other appetizer that looked good was the duck rillet, and even for me that seemed like a lot of duck. The gazpacho was smooth and tasty, topped with lightly fluffed mozzarella. My duck breast was perfectly cooked, with a delicious sauce. There were little mounds of souffled sides, I think one was sweet peas and the other cauliflower, which I thought were good but Steve practically licked his plate. In this case, the presentation of the dishes was well thought-out (though not as over-the-top as Le Cottage), and the food was phenomenal. Across the board, everyone in our party raved about their food, and we left replete.

On our second visit, my mom and I considered splitting the tuna ravioli, but after a brief consultation with Carole, the owner, we decided the chef's specialty of home-made duck liver terrine poached with red wine, cinnamon and spices would do the trick even better. My mom is not generally a fan of foie gras, but after a week and a half in Grand Case and exposure to proper duck liver, I think she's coming around. I ordered the beef tenderloin with goat cheese and truffle panad, while my mother opted for the pork tenderloin smoked with cigar in vanilla sauce. We weren't entirely certain how the latter would be accomplished – would a cigar make an appearance? – and we

Mood	
Romance	★★★★★
Relaxation	★★★★★
Fun	★★★★★
Family	★★★☆☆
Value	★★★★☆

Food	
Taste	★★★★★
Innovation	★★★★★
Display	★★★★★
Drinks	★★★★★

Service	
Attentive	★★★★★
Speed	★★★★★
Knowledge	★★★★★

Atmosphere	
Views	★★★☆☆
Decor	★★★★★
Comfort	★★★★★
Noise	★★★★★

were intrigued enough to want an answer.

Even before the appetizer, we were impressed by the warm cumin bread rolls with truffle butter, an unexpectedly tasty combination. When the foie gras arrived, all conversation ceased. Lucky for my mom, they had already split the appetizer into separate, meticulously crafted plates,

Foie Gras

When the main course arrived, the mystery of the cigar-smoked pork tenderloin was solved in a dramatic fashion. Though the cigar doesn't come to the table (I mean come on, they're French, not Cuban), the pork arrives with a glass cloche trapping the cigar smoke, which Carole ceremoniously removes so that you can get a whiff of the aromatic smoke. Perhaps if others knew about these magical vanilla cigars, the Cuban economy would be in better shape, but I digress. My mom's reaction to the pork: food of the gods. An unusual but utterly perfect blending of a whiff of smoke and a hint of vanilla.

otherwise she would not have received anywhere close to her fair share... and I'm pretty sure she's now decided she likes foie gras. The foie gras was perfectly smooth, with just that hint of port wine at the edges, and a sprinkle of sea salt. But to top it off, there was an inspired addition of a few morsels of popcorn, and cinnamon-infused granita, which together put us over the edge of culinary bliss.

My filet was perfectly prepared, and topped with just the right amount of goat cheese, perfectly moist and melted without being gushy, and a healthy serving of truffle tapenade. As I ate each bite, there was precisely the right amount of cheese and truffle to complement the filet. Unlike many French restaurants who rely heavily on the sauce to cover any

Filet with goat cheese and truffles

imperfections in the rest of the dish, in this case the dash of sauce was exactly in proportion to augment and highlight the rest of the flavors instead of overwhelm it.

Last time at L'Estaminet, I noticed that all dishes came with the same souffled side dishes, which is kind of nice because it avoids extensive arguments over sharing or the lack thereof. This time around, we both had the same sides, but they have stepped up their vegetable game considerably. There were tiny-diced carrots with cinnamon, zucchini with South American almond, sauteed mushrooms, mashed potatoes that were so perfectly cooked that they didn't even need butter or cream and broccoli that was infused with what seemed like lemongrass, and made me want to cry. When Carole came by to check on us, I could only sniffle and reply " There are no words."

Throughout this remarkable repast, everything was complemented by a phenomenal, reasonably priced gigondas red wine. When Carole consulted with us on our wine choice, she kindly offered to pour it by the glass instead of having to purchase an entire bottle.

When it came time to consider dessert, my mother was close to tears, and said she thought we shouldn't order dessert, because what if it ruins our perfect meal? But we were feeling lucky, so we doubled down and ordered the creme brulee assortment. Chocolate. Lime. Ginger. Who would have suspected these would brulee so well? Apparently Ina the genius chef did, because they were a delight.

To top it all off, and send us out into the night better women than when we started, Carole served up their signature digestif. Not rum. Oh no, nothing so traditional for this innovative gem. Rather, it's a multi-layered extravaganza of kahlua, then Baileys, then cream (heavy, to be sure) and liberally sprinkled with cocoa. Carole instructed us that we must drink it as a shot, no sippies. Zing! Et voila. A perfect ending to one of the most remarkably delicious meals I've ever had the pleasure to enjoy.

Magical digestif

Dining room

Service at L'Estaminet

The service at L'Estaminet is solid, in so many ways.

On our first visit, remember we were having a bit of a party? Well, after we had eaten well, and drunk more than our fair share... I can admit it now... we started getting a little rowdy. I have been told that my voice carries, and for some reason carries more when I've been drinking (surprise, surprise). As it turns out, our new friend is similarly endowed. We were getting some rather dirty looks from the French couple across the way. This is where I give our hostesses a lot of credit. Instead of tossing us out, they were kind and apologetic when they conveyed the disturbance, and brought us another round of digestif to soften the blow (which may have exacerbated the issue, but seemed like the right idea at the time).

Carole's finesse ensured both tables were happy with the outcome.

On our second visit, Carole was again the epitome of a gracious hostess. She and Ina, the brilliant chef, are the co-owners, and it's clear from the moment you arrive that they are both passionate about this labor of love. It shows in the food, and it comes out loud and clear in the experience. Carole subtly and effortlessly guided us to the best possible order for our palate. Whenever we might have needed something, she was always there, a half second before we realized. Even when the intimate dining room filled up later in the evening, she was somehow in eight places at once, keeping everyone happy. We watched her brilliantly cater to a table with three little girls, bringing them three perfect little chocolate mousses. When we scarfed down her digestif before remembering to take a photo, she happily brought us another serving... perhaps I should have "forgotten" again?

All told, I felt that the owners and staff cared deeply about making sure that every one of their patrons enjoyed their time at their beautiful little restaurant. By the end of the evening, I felt like we were old friends. You know how there are times when you have a wonderful meal, and though the food is satisfying, the overall experience leaves you cold? Like they were just going through the motions? This was the exact opposite experience. The warm, embracing service added a magical je ne sais quoi to an already superb meal.

Atmosphere at L'Estaminet

Though I often lament the lack of views for the less fortunate restaurants on the "wrong" side of Grand Case Boulevard, I must admit that I think this makes them work harder than their naturally endowed counterparts. If you didn't know there were beautiful views to be had a mere stone's throw across the street, you would never feel anything was missing at L'Estaminet, and even knowing it you don't feel the lack. It is an intimate restaurant, meticulously appointed with art and decor. The view out to the boulevard is perfectly obstructed with tropical plants, enough so that the view is enhanced but the breeze still flows freely. The tables and chairs are comfortable and inviting. Though we were ourselves a bit rowdy on our first visit, on our return trip we found it to be a romantic, relaxing environment in which to enjoy a thoroughly delicious meal (even if it was with my mother).

Bottom Line

Though L'Estaminet is a petit restaurant lacking in views, it more than makes up for it in warmth of welcome and perfectly prepared, delicious food. If I had only one meal to eat in Grand Case, and I absolutely had to choose... which would be really, really cruel because there are some phenomenal options who provide stiff competition... L'Estaminet would be at the top of my list.

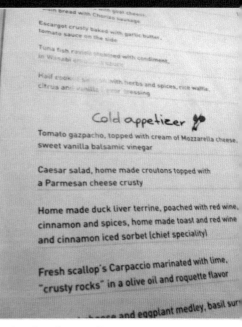

Extensive, innovative menu

Gigondas by the glass

Just the Facts

Price Level:
$$$$$

Category:
French

Meals Served:
Dinner

Location:
97 Grand Case
Boulevard

Phone:
0590 29 03 30

Credit Cards:
Visa

Website:
restaurantlecott
age.com

Currency:
Market rate

Outdoor
seating:
Balcony on
street

Parking:
Nearby lot

Good for:
Foodies, Groups

Pros

Tasting Fooding is a great way to
sample an extensive menu

Grand Marnier Souffles,
Chocolate Souffles, oh my!

Beautifully presented food

Cons

Presentation a little over the top

Le Cottage
Overall Rating ★★★★★

On the non-sea side of Grand
Case Boulevard, you will find a
welcoming, fancy little restaurant
called Le Cottage. It is definitely
one of the nicest on the boulevard,
despite not having water views.
We went there with our friends from
L'Esplanade, and had a fantastic
evening. Of course, being there
with the owners of the hotel
definitely had its perks – the owner
of the restaurant greeted us all
personally, and we got the royal
treatment. However, I got the
impression that the service is
excellent regardless.

The second time we visited Le
Cottage, it was with a group of six
women, most of whom live here in
Grand Case full time. It was low
season, and we had been hearing
about an innovative new offering
called "tasting fooding." With a
name like that, we had to check it
out.

Food at Le Cottage

During high season, the menu was extensive, and heavily favored French haute cuisine with a light island touch. For appetizer, I had the tuna sashimi; it came complete with fried ginger, a treat I will definitely be looking to repeat. The tuna had been sliced very thin, and then rolled on itself, making a perfect tasty bite. Steve shamelessly mooched off my appetizer instead of ordering his own. For main course, I ordered the scallops, and they were tasty as well, though not quite as memorable as Steve's filet, which I "shared" with him every time he got busy talking to people.

Several people ordered the escargot, and it looked amazing. There were six escargot in their individual cups, each topped with a little piece of toast, plus there was a lollipop of foie gras. Really, a lollipop – foie gras at the end of a stick, standing tall on the plate. It was excellent, as long as you didn't actually eat it as a lollipop – it was very good once it was spread on toast. I was starting to really wish I had ordered one of the several foie gras appetizer options. I got the impression that not everyone at our table of eight loved their food, but overall, the consensus seemed to be a solid A minus.

The wine, on the other hand, was a solid A plus. Amazing Chateau Margaux they recommended. Crazy, crazy good, and they just kept bringing it.

Then again, the highlight was without a doubt dessert. We split two souffles, chocolate and Grand Marnier. They were crazy good. I have a feeling I had more than my

Mood	
Romance	★★★★★
Relaxation	★★★★☆
Fun	★★★★★
Family	★★☆☆☆
Value	★★★☆☆

Food	
Taste	★★★★★
Innovation	★★★★★
Display	★★★★★
Drinks	★★★★★

Service	
Attentive	★★★★★
Speed	★★★★☆
Knowledge	★★★★★

Atmosphere	
Views	★★☆☆☆
Decor	★★★★☆
Comfort	★★★☆☆
Noise	★★★★☆

fair share of both. Many people will tell you to order the souffles at Le Cottage. Listen. We know whereof we speak!

The truly memorable aspect of Le Cottage was the presentation of food. Every dish was artfully turned out, with some crazy highlight, like a beaker of froth or the foie gras lollipop. Impressive across the board.

Seafood Tasting

When we visited Le Cottage for the Tasting Fooding in August, we were even further wowed. After the six of us were seated in an appropriately segregated alcove – they were prescient in guessing our inevitable cackling and shrillness would eventually drive other patrons away

Escargot

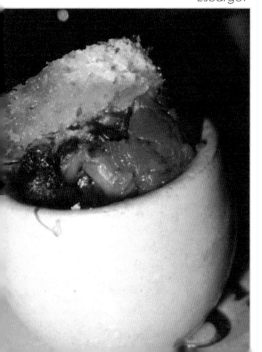

– Bruno began to excitedly explain their new approach. On the left side of the menu, a list of 20 cold appetizers. On the right hand side, 20 hot appetizers. For 18 euro, you get to choose five cold or five hot or five combined. For two people, they would recommend splitting one assortment of cold, then order two assortments of hot, one for each of you. It is an innovative approach, but in fact it took us a little while to understand the explanation, so we simply put ourselves in Bruno's ever-so-capable hands, and allowed him to work with the chef to craft us an amazing tasting experience.

When the platters arrived, filled with an expansive assortment of goodies of all colors and concoctions, we didn't really know where to start... we looked at each other, waited to see who would blink first, shrugged, and dug in.

And OMG! Every single thing we tasted was delicious. Our favorite was what we renamed the "Fluffy Duck," which as far as we could tell was duck tartare in a little mug, filled to the brim with magical duck-infused, creme fraiche-based, creamy froth. There was a small tomato stuffed with a burrata mozzarella cheese filling – it was a perfect bite that must have taken 10 minutes alone to hand craft. There were beakers of different flavored (and multi-colored) gazpacho, topped with sprout confetti, and complete with straws to facilitate sharing. The whole presentation made me feel like a science geek kid who has just received his first chemistry set and can't wait to discover the joy of blowing up the basement. One of my personal favorites was the foie gras lollipop, crusted in pepper. We must have tried tastes of 30+ dishes, and not a single one fell short in either taste or presentation. The best part is we now each have a short list of dishes we want to order next time we go! Sadly, the Fooding Tasting is only for low season (I'm hoping they change their mind about that), so if you're here when it's available, I highly recommend it.

After the hot tasting, we decided we were happily full without being stuffed, a nice feeling, and therefore perfect for ordering several desserts. On our last visit to Le Cottage, I was introduced to the Grand Marnier souffle, and it was an absolute must order. And now they have a caramel souffle? Sign me up. Oh, AND there is a dessert fooding tasting? Yeah, that too. By the end it looked like there had been a sweet massacre, or at least a sacrifice offered up to the goddess of girlie feasting.

Atmosphere at Le Cottage

Le Cottage may be on the "wrong" side of Grand Case Boulevard, i.e. not overlooking the Caribbean, but they have attempted to make up for it in carefully decorating the interior. The dining room is wide open to the boulevard to create an airy, open flow, but without feeling like you're being run down by a car or bus. There are only a handful of tables – it's a relatively small restaurant – so it feels very intimate. The color scheme of cherry and gray, with splashes of creamy yellow was absolutely lovely; the restaurant would not be out of place on a Paris street.

Tomato stuffed with Burrata

The table they provided our party of six women was perfect – still part of the main dining room, but slightly set off to the side in an alcove. The walls are heavily painted and sculptured to ensure even the most raucous ladies night won't interrupt the enjoyment of other diners.

Dessert Tasting

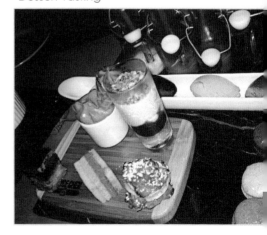

Le Cottage balcony

Service at Le Cottage

The service was definitely impeccable, though again, I must reiterate that we were there with owners of the Hotel L'Esplanade who knew the owners of Le Cottage, so we were without a doubt given the star treatment. On our second trip, we were also there with people known to the restaurants, so again, perhaps we have been spoiled. But I have to say – putting ourselves in Bruno's capable hands on both occasions paid extensive dividends. Our friends who live here also rave about the service.

One of the servers noticed that one of our Gaggle of Six was sneezing from allergies. He immediately brought her a paper handkerchief, and then gave each of the rest of us one as well. How thoughtful is that? We had two servers for the six of us, and we were never without filled water or wine glasses. This was French service at its best.

My mom, aka "Grey Squirrel," (though, for the record, she hasn't let her grey hair show EVER), had this to add: "It's wonderful having good food on vacation, but it's even more wonderful to have a memorable total dining experience encompassing ambience, food, conversation and service. Our Fooding Tasting at Le Cottage was

Meeting of the Secret Squirrels

indeed memorable, one of my favorite dinners ever!"

Bottom line

I've rarely, if ever, seen the kind of meticulous artistry that the chef of Le Cottage puts into every delicious bite. If you love innovative, artistic French cuisine, try Le Cottage, you're in for an amazing treat. Here's hoping they decide to keep the Tasting Fooding all year round.

Trust Bruno

Whether you are having the tasting menu, or trying to decide on a wine pairing, Bruno is your guy - he will steer you in the right direction!

Grammatically challenged? yes. Gastronomically challenged? Not in the least.

Unbeatable Souffle

Just the Facts

Price Level:
$$$$$

Category:
French

Meals Served:
Dinner

Location:
89 Grand Case
Boulevard

Phone:
0590 87 73 37

Credit Cards:
Visa

Website:
laubergegourm
ande.com

Currency:
Market rate

Outdoor seating:
Balcony on street

Parking:
Nearby lot

Good for:
Foodies, Groups

Pros

The Grande Dame of Grand Case, Auberge helped start it all 30 years ago

Earth-shatteringly delicious food

Perfect service

Cons

No water views

L'Auberge Gourmande
Overall Rating ★★★★★

It was almost thirty years ago that L'Auberge Gourmande appeared on the Grand Case scene to usher in the era of the Gourmet Capital of the Caribbean. Prior to the arrival of three seminal restaurants, of which L'Auberge is one, the small fishing village was just that. Now look what they started! In a charming 120 year old Creole-style house, L'Auberge Gourmande is the Grande Dame of Grand Case, still serving up innovative, delicious haute cuisine that continues to set the standard.

We missed L'Auberge on our first visit, opting for the newer restaurants, and I am incredibly relieved we rectified that omission on our second trip. Unlike most restaurants we review, we only had one meal at L'Auberge, but it was sufficiently amazing to warrant a review. We will not make the mistake of missing L'Auberge on future trips.

Food at L'Auberge Gourmande

I'll admit, I was hard-pressed to make a decision at L'Auberge. The menu had so many mouthwatering options, I found myself mulling far longer than normal as I savored the lovely bottle of Sancerre. Lobster? Cote d'agneau? Mahi mahi? Or go with the filet de boeuf with my *choice* of poivre or roquefort or shallot or morel sauce? Well, clearly I had to go with the filet de boeuf, "cooked for my convenience" according to the menu. After some cajoling, I convinced my mother that we clearly had to order the seared foie gras for appetizer, even though she doesn't technically consider herself a fan. She then opted for the Chilean sea bass and shrimp with coconut sauce.

First, the foie gras appeared, complete with a perfect fan of poached pears and a light sauterne sauce drizzled over the entire plate. The foie gras was perfectly seared – warmed without being cooked – and spread smoothly on the freshly baked, still warm rolls that appeared as if my magic. There was not one, but two healthy slabs of foie gras awaiting our attention. But wait, there's more. Underneath the foie gras, there were lightly crusted slices of baguette, sitting atop – surprise! – a light sweet potato puree. Together with the pears and sauterne sauce the effect was mind-blowingly delicious. I had high hopes that my mom, not being a "fan," would let me have more than my fair share, but I found myself having to fight for every morsel.

And then, the entrees arrived. My mother described her Chilean sea

Mood	
Romance	★★★★★
Relaxation	★★★★★
Fun	★★★★☆
Family	★★☆☆☆
Value	★★★☆☆

Food	
Taste	★★★★★
Innovation	★★★★☆
Display	★★★★☆
Drinks	★★★★☆

Service	
Attentive	★★★★★
Speed	★★★★☆
Knowledge	★★★★☆

Atmosphere	
Views	★★☆☆☆
Decor	★★★★★
Comfort	★★★★☆
Noise	★★★☆☆

bass as delicate, meltingly good, and absolutely divine. Possibly one of the best fish dishes she's ever had. And then I had to listen to her make sounds that no daughter should ever be subjected to, much less in public.

My filet... well, ok, let me start by saying that it turns out what ensued was all my fault. I studied French in high school, studied it in college, spent a semester at Universite de

Sea Bass

Grenoble, then went back for an internship in Paris my junior year, visited a few times after that. But I never actually had any money when I was a student, so while my French is passably decent (or so I am told, especially by drunk Frenchmen), my familiarity with haute cuisine terms hasn't yet caught up.

So... I had ordered my filet "a point." A point. I was certain this meant medium rare. And I have to tell you, I love me a good rare steak. I can't stand overcooked beef. Why bother if you're going to kill all the flavor? But apparently there are differences of interpretation of "a point." Somewhere along the way, I was misinformed. Mistakes were made. Suffice it to say that, having insisted on showing off my French, I ordered "a point." What arrived at the table had passed the point of pink, which means it was well past my idea of acceptable.

When I waved the waiter over and told him I had ordered medium rare, he was horrified by what he saw, apologized profusely, and

immediately whisked away my plate. The waitress who had taken my order then came by and also apologized profusely.

At this point, mortification set in, and it occurred to me that perhaps it had been my translation error... and so I asked in English what is medium rare in French. Apparently the widely accepted translation is "saignant." Doh! Yeah, that would be my bad. But let me tell you. They were as considerate and apologetic and handled it as elegantly as I've ever seen a restaurant handle even their own mistake, much less a customer's.

Within minutes my saignant filet de boeuf appeared. The side dishes were clearly fresh – none of that re-heat the original business from these guys! And the filet, oh the filet, was utter perfection. Brilliant cut of meat. Perfect medium rare, on the bloody side the way I like it, but not too much so. The sauce! Ooh la la. The sauce was buttery and peppery and rich and flavorful and all the wonderful things God intended a proper poivre sauce to be. Now, some might say it was a mere one shake short of too much salt, but for me, it brought out the depth of flavors perfectly. Artistically arrayed around the plate, I found three spears of crisp asparagus, a single floret of broccoli, a perfectly roasted tomato provencal (tomato stuffed with garlicky goodness), a cauliflower and cheese souffle... and one of the best potatoes au gratin I've experienced in a long time. It was a smorgasbord of French earthly delights.

Dessert? Impossible. We searched the depths of our stomachs and found they had been so superbly filled there was simply no way for us to do justice to the tempting array of treats on the dessert menu. I mean, how do you pass up an au delice with layers of creme brulee and chocolate mousse? We vowed, practically signed in blood, that we would return for dessert one night soon, which sadly wasn't possible. Now that I've seen the desserts on their web site, I am despondent thinking of what we missed! Next trip.

And so they brought us their signature banana vanilla caramel rum digestif. Many places tell you they offer banana vanilla rum, but like the restaurant itself, this rum set the bar. Darker and thicker than your average rum digestif.

Service at L'Auberge Gourmande

L'Auberge Gourmande is a family affair. Unlike many of the restaurants that have changed hands over the years, L'Auberge Gourmande has stayed in the family. Our charming waitress, Candace, said she's been working there for 21 years... which is remarkable since she looks like she's only 21. Turns out she started there when she was eight. Her father, Pascal, came by a couple times over the course of the evening to check on us as well, as did David, who is a relative newcomer to the restaurant.

As I mentioned, the aplomb with which they handled the steak snafu was, in a word, impressive. Beyond that, they were the picture of professional French service. They were there when you needed them, poured your wine just as the realization that you wanted a refill barely started to knock at your consciousness, and steered you just right with knowledgeable, well-informed guidance on the menu.

Atmosphere at L'Auberge Gourmande

It's like sitting down to dinner at an old friend's house, one who has lived in her house for generations and carefully accumulated all the objets d'art to make her carefully constructed room feel effortless. The bright yellow faux finish on the walls perfectly offsets the heavy wood box beam ceiling. White archways and shuttered doors separate you from the traffic of the boulevard, without cutting you off from the evening breezes. Intimate, with comfortable seating. Never any issues with noise, even when the dining room filled up.

Bottom line

Beyond the tangible, tantalizing food... at L'Auberge Gourmande you can feel the history, the gossamer weight of 30 years of culinary excellence. L'Auberge Gourmande is not to be missed.

Dining room

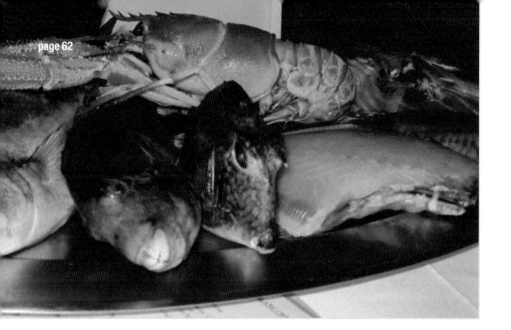

Just the Facts

Price Level:
$$$$

Category:
Seafood

Meals Served:
Breakfast,
Dinner

Location:
48 Grand Case
Boulevard

Phone:
0590 87 05 65

Credit Cards:
Visa

Currency:
market rate

Outdoor
seating:
water view

Parking:
Nearby lot

Good for:
Everyone

Pros

Best assortment of fresh local fish in Grand Case, all exquisitely prepared

Small, intimate dining room with perfect sunset views

Roman provides exceptional

Cons

Can get a little warm

Le Ti Provencal
Overall Rating ★★★★☆

On the beach side of Grand Case boulevard is a small, but wonderful place to go for fresh, local fish, cooked and served to perfection. Herve is both the chef and the owner, and opened Le Ti Provencal about 6 years ago, after cooking at locations throughout France. He is ably assisted by waiter and master fish-deboner Roman.

My mom and I went to Le Ti Provencal on the recommendation of several locals, arriving after a late afternoon thunderstorm had lowered the steamy temperatures a little bit and created cloud formations promising a spectacular sunset. Roman greeted us, and seated us at a small table perfect for watching the technicolor show over the water. At just before 7pm on a Saturday in August, we were the only patrons.

Food at Le Ti Provencal

Our first impression of the food was when Roman brought out the traditional French chalkboard menu; why bother with printed menus when you change your menu based on what was caught that morning? He left it propped on a chair from the neighboring table, and my mom and I perused and discussed, and arrived at a plan.

But that plan went out the window. Roman arrived carrying a tray of, yes, dead fish. Which sounds really, really gross... but somehow it wasn't. They were fresh. Even in the Caribbean heat, standing with the platter next to me, not only was there no fishy smell, it was more like the fresh tang of the sea had walked to my table. For that matter, you'd think it might skeeve you out, all those eyes staring at you, and we Americans aren't really used to that sort of thing. But it didn't. Then the real treat came when Roman walked us through each of the fish, their preparation options, how they taste, texture, everything you needed to know. We quickly ditched our plan when we realized the true menu was in Roman's head, and on that platter. I've never before had a waiter so thoroughly help select the exact best meal for me.

After extensive analysis, my mother and I decided to split the warm trunk fish salad for an appetizer, then I would have the sea bream grilled with Creole sauce, while she would have the trigger fish filet, au meuniere style. I was torn on the trunk fish because, as a diver, I know how cute they are when you see them swimming around Creole Rock. I mean, it's got cute little

Mood	
Romance	★★★★★
Relaxation	★★★★★
Fun	★★★★☆
Family	★★★☆☆
Value	★★★★☆

Food	
Taste	★★★★★
Innovation	★★★☆☆
Display	★★★★☆
Drinks	★★★★☆

Service	
Attentive	★★★★★
Speed	★★★★★
Knowledge	★★★★★

Atmosphere	
Views	★★★★★
Decor	★★★☆☆
Comfort	★★☆☆☆
Noise	★★★★☆

horns. In fact, all of the fish at Le Ti Provencal are so local that, if you've been on a dive, you have seen them, and in fact may have met that exact fish. But you get past it.

When the warm trunk fish salad arrived, kindly partitioned into two bowls, we were in seafood nirvana. Seriously, I've never had a salad like this. The trunk fish was indeed warm

Warm trunk fish salad

– exactly warm, not hot, not cold. I think it might have been poached and then shredded, because it didn't even look like fish per se, it was so light and smooth in texture. If you've never had trunk fish, it is indeed a lot like chicken, very tasty, light chicken. Along with the fish, there was butter lettuce and a carefully diced assortment of tomatoes, herbs and aromatics, all perfectly blended in a light oil and lemon dressing. It was delightfully refreshing.

Sea Bream and Trigger Fish

For the main course, Roman had kindly offered to split both the sea bream and trigger fish so that my mother and I would each have half and half. Perfect. But first, he brought the full fish out to the table so we could observe a master de-boner at work. It was impressive! Not a single bone was found in our meal.

The fish? Oh, the fish! Both were perfectly cooked, so that they were moist and tender and flaked apart on your fork, no knife necessary, but still with a thin crisp skin for that extra texture. The sea bream was light, and when dipped in the Creole sauce – essentially melted butter with an assortment of aromatics blended in, not spicy, just flavorful – it was delicious. The trigger fish had been done au meuniere, so it was mildly pan fried and garnished with a buttery lemon sauce, and again the light sauce perfectly complemented it. At the end of it, we were exquisitely satisfied, not over-stuffed, so we had room for dessert!

Like many of the other restaurants on Grand Case Boulevard, Le Ti Provencal offered a chocolate lava cake, but in keeping with the theme of a light tropical meal, we instead opted for the lemon tarte. Mon Dieu! The meringue!! It was phenomenal. Extremely light, even though it had the thickest, tastiest layer of freshly whipped meringue I have ever tasted. Still warm.

After our tasty tarte, we opted for a cup of tea, for which they had a broad assortment of options, and a clever little teapot/cup ensemble. The rum digestif arrived, and it was again light and unusual: cashew flavored. Our meal was perfectly paired with a crisp pouilly fume.

What impressed me most about the meal at Le Ti Provencal was its sheer lack of pretense or subterfuge. It was perfectly cooked, thoughtfully presented, but I could probably count the number of ingredients for each dish on one hand. There was nothing for the fish to hide behind, it had to be perfect. In some ways it might appear to be the antithesis of innovation – something I often prize – but it was so expertly and honestly prepared, with the freshest local ingredients, it won us over. I do not in any way mean to impugn Herve's masterful skills as a chef – the exact opposite. Sometimes the simplest ideas turn out the best.

Beautiful views

Service at Le Ti Provencal

Roman was the only waiter working in the restaurant, and he spent copious amounts of time with each table, and yet he kept everything running smoothly. His attention to detail and knowledge were unparalleled. We had a lengthy discussion as to what seafood is and isn't local to St. Martin; turns out shrimp aren't, and I was heartbroken, though I shouldn't have been surprised, I was just in denial. But I digress. After my mom and I had made menu decisions, our discussion with Roman steered us in all new directions, and we were extremely glad with the end result. Not only was he exceedingly knowledgeable, he was just warm and engaging. High marks all around.

Atmosphere at Le Ti Provencal

What can I say, Le Ti Provencal is one of the "haves" on Grand Case

Boulevard. Whereas some restaurants use this as an excuse to skimp on the food, owner Herve takes the opposite tack. The decor is simple: decorated in the bright blues, yellows and reds of Provence in such a way that embraces and highlights the natural beauty without attempting to compete. It's a small, intimate dining room, and there was only one other table that came in during our early Saturday night dinner.

My only *minor* complaint is that it was a bit humid on the evening we were there, and the dining room would have benefited from more than one fan. A ceiling fan would not be a wasted investment.

Bottom line

At the end of the day, if you're looking for a quiet, relaxing, romantic spot to enjoy the best local seafood on St. Martin, simply prepared yet wonderfully executed, Le Ti Provencal is the perfect restaurant.

Just the Facts

Price Level: $$$$	Credit Cards: Visa
Category: French	Currency: 1 $ = 1 euro
Meals Served: Dinner	Outdoor seating: none
Location: 93 Grand Case Boulevard	Parking: Nearby lot
Phone: 0590 52 36 59	Good for: Foodies, Groups
Website: lavillasxm.com	

Pros

Chocolate lava cake! Delicious pumpkin cappuccino; phenomenal filet au poivre

Beautifully plated, innovative food combinations

Comfortable, breezy dining room

Cons

Service a little slow when busy

La Villa
Overall Rating ★★★★☆

Reviewed by Madam J and Marc AuMarc, residents extraordinaire of Grand Case, St. Martin

When Alain, the bartender at Hotel L'Esplanade and a second-generation resident of Grand Case, picked Lucinda and her mom up at the airport, she knew he was the perfect person to ask: "which is your favorite gourmet restaurant on the Boulevard?" His response? La Villa. He recommended Le Cottage and L'Auberge as well, but his favorite was La Villa, a relative newcomer to the Boulevard. Reason? The chocolate fondue cake, of course!

La Villa is a relative newcomer to the Grand Case strip of gourmet spots, and we'd given it a whirl during the growing pains of its first few months open. Longtime St.

Martin visitors and residents will know it as the space of the former L'Alabama. When we returned with Lucinda and her mom Vicki, we were pleased to find that La Villa has ironed out most of the kinks. If you're looking for a leisurely French dinner in an elegant Caribbean setting, La Villa definitely fits the bill.

Food at La Villa

Expect a solid menu ranging from French classics with an island twist to some more innovative creations, and daily specials. The 49€ prix fixe menu offers a more reasonable way for foodies, famished, or both to taste their way through three courses–so naturally, we went for it.

La Villa boasts a fine list of French wines from quite a range of regions at diverse price points, and there's also a full bar. We savored an absolutely ravishing Sancerre (the "Les Baronnes" 2008 Henri Bourgeois) for 39€, and then savored it again when we agreed another bottle was clearly necessary.

With our first glasses of wine, amuse bouche of black olive tapenade with anchovy served with little toasts were presented, followed by a selection of bread and a crock of butter. La Villa passed the key "Madam J Butter Test" with flying colors.

Our appetizers arrived looking beautiful. The standout plate was absolutely Vicki's Caribbean pumpkin cappuccino with sweet potato chips. The rest of us were a bit jealous after a spoonful each of the airy, creamy, savory soup. Vicky commented that that type of richly nuanced flavor is very hard to achieve. She was surprised that the

Mood	
Romance	★★★★☆
Relaxation	★★★★★
Fun	★★★☆☆
Family	★★★★☆
Value	★★★★☆

Food	
Taste	★★★★☆
Innovation	★★★★☆
Display	★★★★★
Drinks	★★★★★

Service	
Attentive	★★★★☆
Speed	★★★☆☆
Knowledge	★★★★☆

Atmosphere	
Views	★☆☆☆☆
Decor	★★★★★
Comfort	★★★★☆
Noise	★★★★☆

chips weren't crisp, but found them very natural tasting and a delicious way to showcase the true flavor of sweet potato–a lovely complement to the pumpkin soup. The other appetizers were more uneven. Lucinda chose the sea scallop ravioli with bisque emulsion. She found the bisque light and creamy without being too heavy, but although the ravioli were freshly made, it wasn't the best pasta: the

Seared Duck

slightly burnt–tragedy! But the amazing sauce helped rescue it, and the seeds added a pleasantly unusual texture. Marc's duck egg roll with orange and ginger sauce was enjoyable, competently executed and crispy with a tangy-sweet sauce, but he didn't find it super-flavorful and would have loved more ginger.

Our main courses were superb. Lucinda's duck breast with foie gras millefeuille and porto wine sauce was a glorious work of millefeuille fabulousness. Though she initially asked for the duck medium rare, she noted that the rare slices that arrived were fantastically cooked and just right for the dish. Other raves were the phenomenal port wine sauce for its zing and depth of flavor, the foie gras–here perfectly done–and "the piece of bread below that receives all goodness coming down!" Vicki was likewise thrilled by her red snapper filet roll with bacon-stuffed sea scallops and pink peppercorn sauce. She praised the appealing presentation, the melange of flavors with "a subtle spice that's not too spicy" and the expert use of the bacon's saltiness to balance the dish. She was impressed by the way the chef married the textures and demands of bacon and fish–"It's tricky to cook both!"–and really liked that she could choose how much of the herb-infused sauce to add.

skin was veering a bit towards chewy, as if it had been cooked a bit too long. Overall, it was not as complex and flavorful as she'd expected. My sautéed foie gras with apple chutney and cherry vinegar was overcooked, even

Filet au Poivre

My angus beef filet with 5 pepper sauce flambéed with cognac was tender and cooked to order, with a creamy sauce that was scrumptious but also unexpectedly spicy! Lushly savory potatoes au gratin rounded out a solid plate. Marc definitely enjoyed his rack of lamb baked

with goat cheese and zucchini cake. The flavorful, perfectly cooked richness of the lamb was excellently offset by the gorgeous goat cheese and a tasty, not-too-sweet honey and rosemary sauce. The light yellow squash and zucchini gratin cake was lovely–meltingly soft, not overwhelmingly rich but with a good creaminess. "The squash really comes through–they avoided the temptation to over-season."

For dessert, everyone except me decided on the molten chocolate lava cake served with vanilla ice cream, a specialty of the house. This gorgeous creation of hot, velvety, dense dark chocolate, with a deliciously melty center, was insanely good. I opted for the tiramisu, but something was off–Lucinda and I were startled by a sour, rotten-dairy taste. Maybe the cheese or cream was bad? Our waitress handled it very professionally, explaining that it had been made fresh that day, but also apologizing and immediately removing it from the table (and our bill), and, when I wasn't game to try another dessert, offering us all free after-dinner drinks. We wrapped up with the after-after-dinner drinks: the traditional coconut rum shot.

Service at La Villa

Service was warm, genuinely friendly and attentive, and the wait staff were very knowledgeable about the menu, specials and wine list. They were ready to share suggestions and recommendations, and we never felt rushed. We also noticed that we're always greeted now when we walk by the restaurant. That said, when they're busy they do get stretched a little thin.

Inviting interior

Atmosphere at La Villa

La Villa's gingerbread Creole architecture, wooden shutters, white-painted and dark beadboard wooden walls, and flagstone floors lend an elegantly Caribbean vibe to the restaurant. Chic table settings, a chocolate and white color scheme with orange-red-spice accents and warm, carved-wood décor complete the ambience. They have about 10 well-spaced-out tables, and the seating is wrought-iron chairs with cushions, quite beautiful but not super comfy. The large open-air windows capture the island breezes and make La Villa an excellent spot to watch the Harmony Nights festivities. Overall, romantic, relaxing and fun–though definitely not rowdy.

Bottom Line

Having cut their teeth next door at L'Auberge, Christophe and Francoise demonstrated they have learned what works: outstanding, innovative food, and one of the best chocolate lava cakes on the Boulevard.

Le Tastevin
Overall Rating ★★★★☆

Le Tastevin came highly recommended by the Hotel L'Esplanade staff, as both romantic and yummy, and it lived up to both expectations.

Food at Le Tastevin

In an attempt to be somewhat virtuous, I ordered a simple salad with asparagus and tomatoes to start. It was light and refreshing. Unfortunately for my waistline, Steve has been embracing his newfound love of foie gras. Once I had a taste of it, the barely eaten salad sat untouched, sad and forgotten. Not only was it wonderful foie gras, but it came with a fresh Fig compote and fleur de sel that completed it like Jerry Maguire. It was sinfully delicious.

For our main course, I ordered the duck breast in a 5-spice sauce. The duck was perfectly prepared, the sauce delightful. There were tiny skewers of pineapple, providing a perfect sweet

Just the Facts

Price Level:
$$$$

Category:
French

Meals Served:
Lunch, Dinner

Location:
86 Grand Case Boulevard

Phone:
0590 87 55 45

Credit Cards:
Visa

Currency:
market rate

Outdoor seating:
Water view

Parking:
Nearby lot

Good for:
Foodies, Couples

Pros

Scrumptious, authentic food, especially the Foie Gras

Beautiful scenery, probably one of the best on Grand Case Boulevard

Attentive, knowledgeable service

Cons

Not a quick or inexpensive meal

counterpoint. Steve ordered the filet (no surprise). It had what at first seemed like a traditional French sauce, but ended with a frisky hint of island spice. Very tasty.

We decided to forego dessert in favor of finishing our yummy bottle of Chateau Margaux (yes, we're hooked now).

Service at Le Tastevin

A special note on the service at Le Tastevin: it was exceptional. Though the restaurant was fairly packed by the end of our dinner, we noticed neither noise nor any sense of abandonment. To the contrary, they were perfectly attentive. In fact, the one waiter made a great recommendation of a light, not-too-sweet dessert wine that would perfectly complement the foie gras. We received the perfect balance of service: attentive without being intrusive.

Atmosphere at Le Tastevin

The restaurants on Boulevard Grand Case are divided into those on the side of the boulevard that are open to the beach and waves, and all the rest. Le Tastevin is perfectly situated – it's completely open to the cool breeze, one story above the lapping waves on the beach. Its decor is subtle and tasteful, and designed to embrace the beautiful scenery, which has been perfectly illuminated and framed by lush greenery. Though almost every table was full (on a Wednesday night, no less), it didn't feel crowded at all. The tables are well spaced so as to keep the noise down and create the sensation of a private dinner on the beach.

Mood

Romance	★★★★★
Relaxation	★★★★☆
Fun	★★★★☆
Family	★★★☆☆
Value	★★★★☆

Food

Taste	★★★★☆
Innovation	★★★☆☆
Display	★★★★☆
Drinks	★★★★☆

Service

Attentive	★★★★★
Speed	★★★★★
Knowledge	★★★★★

Atmosphere

Views	★★★★★
Decor	★★★★☆
Comfort	★★★★★
Noise	★★★★★

Bottom Line

Le Tastevin was one of the best balances between spectacular views and top notch gourmet cuisine. I was sad they were closed for the season when my Mom and I returned in August - was looking forward to their foie gras!

Bistrot Caraibes
Overall Rating ★★★★☆

Just the Facts

Price Level:
$$$$

Category:
Seafood

Meals Served:
Dinner

Location:
81 Grand Case
Boulevard

Phone:
0590 29 08 29

Website:
bistrotcaraibes.
com

Credit Cards:
Visa

Currency:
market rate

*Outdoor
seating:*
Water view

Parking:
Nearby lot

Good for:
Foodies,
Couples

Pros

Oh, the lobster with garlic butter!!
Try the half and half, grilled v.
thermidor

Don't miss the pop rocks in the
chocolate lava cake

Calm, mellow atmosphere, A/C!

Cons

No outdoor area or views

Bistrot Caraibes is on the corner of Grand Case Boulevard and Rue des Ecoles, the road that takes you to the boulangerie, as well as the small local grocery store. Bistrot Caraibes is often used as a reference point. But more importantly, you'll hear it referenced when discussing lobster. We were told by several people that Bistrot Caraibes has the best lobster in Grand Case, and given the myriad of lobster tanks on the boulevard, that is no small boast.

In the beginning, I couldn't really bring myself to partake in the lobster. I'm not against it in principle, but I spent so much time photographing them on my dives in the protected waters, it didn't really seem right. But then it happened. On one of my dives near Tintamarre, suddenly this enormous lobster appeared out of nowhere... and chased me. Seriously. Chased me. Which is odd, because usually lobsters huddle in their dark crevices and don't give you the time of day, but boy, this guy had something to prove. Or he had rabies. Because like a raccoon out in the middle of the day, he looked me dead in the eye, raised up his tentacles, yelled "boo!" and charged. I have never flippered so hard, which is, you know, kind of silly in retrospect, since these lobsters don't have pincers and can't actually hurt you. But after that experience, all bets were off. It was time to take my revenge and start sampling the local lobster.

Food at Bistrot Caraibes

On our first visit, we arrived intent on our lobster mission. After being seated, I barely looked at the menu; I already knew what I wanted. But it almost fell apart. After I smugly ordered my lobster, and began sipping my crisp white wine, the waiter returned and asked me to accompany him to the lobster pool. OK, no problem, I strode confidently to the edge of the pool... and then I stood over them, and saw all those lobsters, scurrying over each other, trying to avoid the dreaded Claw. Apparently it's harder to pass a death sentence when it looks you in the eye.

But I persevered, and wow, am I glad I did. The garlic butter! The garlic butter. Oh, the garlic butter. I could have guzzled it straight from the dipping bowl, it was so good. Worth every calorie. There was also a French cream dipping sauce that was out of this world, but I just couldn't stop with the garlic butter. Addictive. The lobster itself was perfectly grilled, not dry, just succulent and moist... perfect for dipping in the garlic butter.

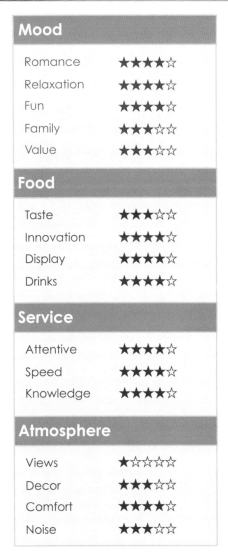

Mood	
Romance	★★★★☆
Relaxation	★★★★☆
Fun	★★★★☆
Family	★★★☆☆
Value	★★★☆☆

Food	
Taste	★★★☆☆
Innovation	★★★★☆
Display	★★★★☆
Drinks	★★★★☆

Service	
Attentive	★★★★☆
Speed	★★★★☆
Knowledge	★★★★☆

Atmosphere	
Views	★☆☆☆☆
Decor	★★★☆☆
Comfort	★★★★☆
Noise	★★★☆☆

Kristin, my mom and I made another visit to Bistrot Caraibes during low season. We each ordered a different appetizer, which we shared amongst us. There was a layered eggplant and crab, warm goat cheese in pastry, or a thousand-layer foie gras. We had mixed reviews on the appetizers: Kristin loved the goat cheese while my mom took a pass. I thought the foie gras was fine, but the pastry accompaniment didn't really do

Lobster - half & half!

much for it. Had I not spent the past two weeks in Grand Case, eating like a queen, they might have impressed me more, but remember, we are grading on a curve here. All were nicely presented and easily gobbled, if not wildly impressive.

Then, on to the entrees... Again, I had the lobster. This time I wasn't subjected to choosing out of the tank, though the proprietor did

Lobster wranglers

bring two over, one in each hand, allowing me to choose. The one in his left was a little feistier, snapping his tail, so I said give him an A for effort, and back in the tank. The quiet one... not so lucky for him, very lucky for me. I was hard-pressed to choose between the traditional island-grilled preparation, and the thermidor approach, which is when they boil the lobster, then remove it from the shell and saute in some magical butter and garlic combination, then put it back in the shell for presentation. Instead of deciding, I opted for the half-and-half option where I got both.

My mom had Thai shrimp with noodles, which was tasty and fairly light. Kristin had grilled sea bass with a Provencal sauce, also tasty. We agreed that the food at Bistrot Caraibes was reliably good, but not astonishingly gourmet. Their signature dish is without a doubt their lobster. If I were grading for the lobster alone.

The big surprise of the evening came with dessert. I know, I sound like a broken record – everyone here does phenomenal dessert. But this was different. The chocolate lava cake with vanilla ice cream was delicious... and then Kristin took her second bite, and turned to me with an incredulous look on her face, and almost jumping out of her chair, cried "Oh My God! Pop Rocks!!" Now, for those of you who don't remember magical pop rocks from your childhood, imagine sugar rock candy crossed with rice crispies, i.e. they go snap crackle pop in your mouth. There were even urban myths about "that kid who died from eating a whole bag of pop rocks and drinking a bottle of coke." (I'm assuming Mythbusters is on it).

Kristin asked the proprietor to confirm, and indeed he admitted they add "Eclats de Sucre Petillants" and showed us the industrial-strength container. I kept expecting to see a bio-hazard symbol. But no, they have made it through France's *rigorous* FDA approval processes, and into the Bistrot Caraibes chocolate lava cake. Shocking. And pure genius. It actually gave the dessert that unexpected, yes, I'm going to say it, *pop*, that we hadn't found elsewhere.

A common landmark

Service at Bistrot Caraibes

If there is one thing you don't want to see when you order lobster, it's the waiter having to spend ten minutes chasing it with a net. Bistrot Caraibes has their pool set up so that they can quickly and efficiently swoop down from above. These guys are professionals. The lobster don't stand a chance. On the other hand, we were treated to an entertaining scene when the staff at the Fish Pot across the street tried their luck in their beautiful but completely impractical lobster tank. Why would you have a huge rock that they can hide behind? At Bistrot Caraibes, there is none of that drama.

Beyond their clear proficiency in lobster wrangling, the staff and owners of Bistrot Caraibes were lovely. The owners are two charming French brothers, Thibault and Amaury, both former chefs in Lyon, and they've been running Bistrot Caraibes for 15 years. At both visits, service was attentive but not pushy. We stayed for hours, chatting with staff and neighboring tables, and never felt we had to leave.

Atmosphere at Bistrot Caraibes

The Bistrot is on the "wrong" side of the boulevard, so don't expect any sunset views over the beach. And it's on a slightly busy corner of the boulevard. And yet... it was perfectly quiet and calm. The lobster pool is a subtle masonry structure, conveniently in between the dining room and the road. The tables and chairs are comfortable and well appointed. The decor is calm and inviting. There is nothing to detract from your enjoyment of a lovely meal.

Bottom line

Bistrot Caraibes isn't my favorite overall gourmet restaurant in Grand Case, but it definitely wins for best lobster. And don't miss the chocolate lava cake with pop rocks!

Spiga
Overall Rating ★★★★☆

A few days after arriving in St. Martin, the first gourmet restaurant we chose to sample in Grand Case was the one closest to Hotel L'Esplanade. A very short walk down the hill (and mercifully brief stumble back), we had heard rave reviews about their purported "creative italian restaurant." Though our last-minute lack of planning meant we had an early-bird 6 p.m. table.

Food at Spiga

We started out by splitting the caprese salad, one of my go-to appetizer choices. With three different stacks of tomato with smooth-as-silk mozzarella (one with avocado, one with olives, one with grilled peppers), it caused us to cease all conversation and focus solely on insuring an impartial allocation of the gustatory booty (not to mention regret having agreed to "splitzies"). After a week of practically becoming a shrimpetarian (they are so fresh and plentiful here), I was craving a little red meat, so we both went in for the filet mignon. It was topped with crumbled blue cheese, and paired with fresh, grilled asparagus and a side of potatoes gratin like only the French truly know how to make. More grilled peppers as garnish, and some sauce drizzled lightly atop everything, completed the dish. Not to mention we paired it with a surprisingly reasonable and refreshing bottle of Barbera d'Alba. Dinner was, in a word: succulent.

Though I'm definitely a carnivore, I have many vegetarian friends, and always keep an eye out for

Just the Facts

Price Level: $$$$	Credit Cards: Visa
Category: Italian	Currency: market rate
Meals Served: Dinner	Outdoor seating: roadside balcony
Location: Rte. de l'Esperance	Parking: Nearby lot
Phone: 0590 52 47 83	Good for: Couples
Website: spiga-sxm.com	

Pros

Tasty, creative Italian food, including excellent filet mignon

Proper italian coffee

Good option for vegetarians

Cons

Don't recommend the outdoor seating; service only so-so

restaurants that effectively cater to them. Though you'll often find seafood options in Grand Case, vegetarian options are harder to come by. Spiga's menu, on the other hand, included several vegetarian options that sounded good even to my red-meat-craving-ears, like the pumpkin-filled ravioli appetizer with butter and sage sauce.

Service at Spiga

Opened in 2002, Spiga is owned by Lara, who plays hostess, and her husband Ciro, the chef. We had heard a lot about how friendly the service was... but alas, we didn't really experience it. We were kind of tucked into a back corner of the dining room, and didn't get much attention at all in terms of water refills, etc. It wasn't bad service per se, just didn't get us excited. In Grand Case in general, you are often greeted by the owners, and we've become accustomed to particularly friendly experiences. Spiga's service was adequate.

Atmosphere at Spiga

Not only is Spiga not on the water side of Grand Case Boulevard, it is unfortunately situated at the point where cars zoom in from the "freeway," before they slow down to a crawl to take the turn into downtown Grand Case. So though there is outdoor seating available at Spiga, I wouldn't recommend it. Not only will you be treated to a view of nothing in particular, you will get the full exhaust and mosquito experience.

That said, the interior of Spiga is lovely. Housed in an authentic Caribbean Creole-style building,

Mood

Romance	★★★★☆
Relaxation	★★★★★
Fun	★★★☆☆
Family	★★★☆☆
Value	★★★★☆

Food

Taste	★★★★★
Innovation	★★★★☆
Display	★★★★☆
Drinks	★★★☆☆

Service

Attentive	★★★☆☆
Speed	★★★☆☆
Knowledge	★★★☆☆

Atmosphere

Views	★☆☆☆☆
Decor	★★★☆☆
Comfort	★★★☆☆
Noise	★★★☆☆

the restaurant is well decorated, comfortable, and inviting. Almost like you're in someone's house, with many thoughtful touches.

Bottom Line

Spiga was one of our first forays into Grand Case gourmet cuisine, and it was delicious, albeit not great service. Good option for vegetarians.

Just the Facts

Price Level:
$$$$$

Category:
French

Meals Served:
Dinner

Location:
94 Grand Case
Boulevard

Phone:
0590 87 75 04

Credit Cards:
Visa

Currency:
market rate

Outdoor seating:
water view

Parking:
Nearby lot

Pros

Spectacular views from an intimate, quiet dining room

Dessert and seafood were excellent - amuse bouche portends yummy soups

Fabulous service

Cons

Duck confit special wasn't so special; No rum digestif offered

L'Escapade
Overall Rating ★★★☆☆

In the interest of completeness, we added L'Escapade to our list of restaurants to check out in Grand Case on our second trip. No one had explicitly recommended it to us, but it was just across the street from some of our favorites (Le Cottage and La Villa). This is the beauty of the gourmet arms race that goes on in Grand Case – no restaurant can survive without striving for excellence, and finding some je ne sais quoi to distinguish it; there are simply too many options. With so many other amazing restaurants, we walked in with slightly lower than usual expectations for a gourmet restaurant on the Boulevard, but determined to seek out L'Escapade's special quality.

Within minutes, our expectations were raised. The black olive tapenade arrived, with just a hint of salty anchovy to mix things up. The glass of sauvignon blanc was refreshing and light. And the view, oh the view! Even for a Grand Case restaurant on the "right" side of the boulevard, L'Escapade surpassed expectations as we watched a perfect sunset.

Food at L'Escapade

The menu at L'Escapade heavily favors seafood, and focuses on traditional French preparations, with some minor notes of island innovation. We had been eating heavily for days by this point, so we thought we'd go light and skip appetizers. My mother went with the coconut-crusted mahi mahi with parmesan risotto and lemongrass foam. Despite my instinct to stick with seafood, I was lured into the duck confit special with portobello mushrooms. Entrees were priced from about 19 euros for vegetarian pasta dishes to almost 40 euros for more expensive cuts of meat.

Before our entrees, we quickly discovered food bliss as the freebies started to arrive. The olive tapenade on croustini was a delicious amuse bouche... and then they brought small cups of butternut squash bisque. Light, flavorful, perfectly balanced flavors, it did much more than amuse us. The hot-from-the-oven rolls arrived, with flaky crust and warm airy insides that instantly melted the traditional French butter. And then the entrees arrived. My mom's fish was lightly cooked, delicately crusted, the flavors appropriately blended, and seasoned just right – not bland, not salty. Flavorful without being heavy. The foam was savory, and packed a punch, but still feather light.

Mood	
Romance	★★★★☆
Relaxation	★★★★☆
Fun	★★★☆☆
Family	★★☆☆☆
Value	★★☆☆☆

Food	
Taste	★★★☆☆
Innovation	★★★☆☆
Display	★★★★☆
Drinks	★★★☆☆

Service	
Attentive	★★★★★
Speed	★★★★★
Knowledge	★★★★☆

Atmosphere	
Views	★★★★★
Decor	★★★★☆
Comfort	★★★★☆
Noise	★★★★★

My duck confit was a little less exciting. The seared portobello mushrooms were a little heavy on the rosemary, and seared slightly more than was strictly necessary in my humble opinion. The duck, while flavorful, was a little stringy... not quite dry, but veering that direction. There wasn't a huge amount of meat, and what there was didn't fall off the bone the way you expect from perfect confit. The

Crepes Suzette

mashed potatoes were yummy, heavy on the butter and cream, and the sauce was flavorful. I had expected more of an olive note based on the description of the special, but there were just a couple scattered around, and they had pits. Overall, it wasn't bad but it also wasn't outstanding, and I've come to expect the extraordinary from the gourmet restaurants on this boulevard.

Dessert, on the other hand, definitely raised the bar. We went wild and crazy and ordered the crepes suzette. They were brought to the table on a platter, with the flaming sauce in a small pitcher to

Mahi Mahi

be poured over top so we could watch the blue flames burn off just enough of the alcohol to warm things up. The sauce was fruity and tangy, the crepes sweet and light. There was a deliciously light puff of cream, along with some home-made vanilla ice cream that seemed to have just a slight hint of anise that gave it a special something. Coupled with some decaf cafe au lait (cafe americain, according to our waitress), it was a redeeming end to the meal. And dessert was indeed the end: contrary to the custom of gourmet restaurants on the boulevard, we were not offered a rum digestif. OK, so that is probably just quibbling, but we did notice the omission.

Service at L'Escapade
Girard, the charming and welcoming owner, opened L'Escapade almost nine years ago. He also now has a restaurant at Cupecoy on the Dutch side called Millennium, and he splits his time between the two. The waitress was particularly enchanting and attentive. She was very astute – when I started speaking French to her, she asked if I would prefer to continue in French and practice, or switch to English. It was the only time I've ever had someone ask me, and I appreciated her inquiring instead of assuming.

Atmosphere at L'Escapade
L'Escapade is one of only a handful of gourmet restaurants blessed with both haute cuisine and sea views. As such, I would definitely say it hit high on the romantic scale. It's an intimate dining room, with six small tables right up at the balcony's edge. The views are spectacular, as

you expect. We arrived just after the sun had set, while there was still the lingering light behind recently released storm clouds, and the result was spectacular.

The dining room itself is bright red with white accents (not the other way around), which might sound off-putting, but in fact comes together for a relatively pleasing ambiance. The chairs definitely rated as some of the most comfortable around, cushioned with high backs, and the airy layout made it a rare senior-friendly destination, especially for someone with mobility issues. There were a few other tables occupied around us, and yet, it was still quiet and intimate. But my favorite part of the L'Escapade ambiance was definitely the music. Frank Sinatra. All night long. I was tempted to join in.

Bottom Line

As one of the few gourmet restaurants also blessed with a seaside view, L'Escapade is a respectable choice in Grand Case, especially for a romantic evening. It wasn't the best or most consistent food we tasted on the Boulevard - foodies may choose to forego the views - but the seafood and dessert delivered, making it a solid option.

Traditional French menu options

Beautiful sunset views

Just the Facts

Price Level:
$$$$$

Category:
French

Meals Served:
Dinner

Location:
17 Grand Case
Boulevard

Phone:
0590 87 07 42

Credit Cards:
Visa

Currency:
1 $ = 1 euro

Outdoor
seating:
none

Parking:
Nearby lot

Pros

Superb seared foie gras with
rosemary pear sauté

Beautiful presentation

1 dollar = 1 euro for cash

Air conditioned!

Cons

Food generally just so-so,
disappointing for such high prices;
Bottled water is a whopping 7

Spicy
Overall Rating ★★☆☆☆

Reviewed by
Madam J and
Marc AuMarc,
residents
extraordinaire of
Grand Case, St.
Martin

Let me get this out of the way
first—there is no spicy food at
Spicy. The "spiciness" is supposed
to be all about the attitude, while
the food is billed as French with a
Mediterranean influence.
Intriguing! We headed to Spicy at
the truly French dinner hour of
8:30 on a hot Monday night,
excited to try a Grand Case
restaurant we'd never been to
before. Spicy is conveniently
located next to the large free
parking lot on the main drag of
Grand Case, across from Zen-It.
We entered the glass doors to be
greeted by the charming co-
owner, Sophie, and a refreshing
wave of A/C, since Spicy is one of
the few (perhaps the only!)

restaurant in town with air-conditioned dining.

The service was excellent and the presentation was exquisite, but overall the food was disappointing, especially at a restaurant that presents itself as a gourmet establishment and charges accordingly. Nothing was really bad–but our takeaway was a resounding "Meh."

Food at Spicy
We were mildly surprised to see that the dinner menu was quite minimal compared to other French gourmet restaurants in town, with only a handful of appetizers and entrees, but this may only be the case in low season. It was supplemented by several fish and seafood specials, which change daily. The English versions of both the menus and the specials board were rife with misspellings and mistranslated wording, which was unintentionally entertaining, but did make it tough to figure out what was on offer. Also, though the wait staff is knowledgeable, we don't think they're aware that there are things the menu isn't clearly communicating to their patrons. Decoding required! One example: I passed on what I thought were simply skewers, based on what I could tell from the menu. Later, we were completely fascinated to spot our waiter affixing a substantial iron stand to a nearby table. It turned out to be the way they suspend their house specialty–meat and seafood served on a GIANT SABER. Wish I'd known that before we ordered! Since we didn't try it, we can't say if it's awesome or just gimmicky, but obviously it would come in handy if you suddenly

Mood
Romance	★★☆☆☆
Relaxation	★★★☆☆
Fun	★★☆☆☆
Family	★☆☆☆☆
Value	★☆☆☆

Food
Taste	★★★☆☆
Innovation	★★★☆☆
Display	★★★★★
Drinks	★★★☆☆

Service
Attentive	★★★★★
Speed	★★★★★
Knowledge	★★★★☆

Atmosphere
Views	★☆☆☆☆
Decor	★★☆☆☆
Comfort	★★★☆☆
Noise	★★★★★

need to challenge anyone to a duel.

We went for the 49 euro (or $49, if you're paying cash with USD) "Spicy Menu" which includes any starter, any entrée, and any dessert. This definitely saves you money if you want all three courses at this pricey venue, but there are two catches: everyone at the table has to do it, and there's a 6 euro surcharge for a

Roasted pepper brie

few of the fancier entrées. Since foie gras is my thing, I went for a double-down: an appetizer pairing of foie gras and the filet mignon Rossini, served with seared foie gras on top, for my entrée. Marc decided on a "roasted pepper brie" starter and the lobster risotto.

Once we'd ordered, our waiter brought out the standard tasty French rolls—and some butter, which unfortunately was completely off. We're not sure if it was actually spoiled, or had just been refrigerated next to something disagreeable, but we steered clear after the first taste. A sad moment for a butter-lover, as the butter

Air conditioned interior

anywhere on the French side is usually absolutely fantastic, and with the usual crusty baguette or roll, provides one of those super-simple yet sublime culinary experiences that typify the island. Luckily Marc had chosen a delicious 2006 Chateau Pay la Tour Bordeaux from their fairly extensive wine list, which helped us readjust.

Our appetizers came out quickly, and, as with everything we saw at Spicy, beautifully presented. Both were plated with a small salad of fresh, crisp mixed greens with vinaigrette. The warm foie gras portion of my foie gras tag-team starter was an absolute standout—it was perfectly seared, melted gorgeously on the tongue, and was marvelously set off by slices of pear sautéed with rosemary and a drizzle of aged balsamic. This was the true highlight of our meal, and the part we can say felt undoubtedly gourmet. As for the other half of the dish, the cold foie gras pate had an odd taste (something afoot with their refrigerator?).

Marc's brie wasn't quite what he'd expected. Rather than a special kind of roasted pepper brie, it was simply three petite chunks of regular brie, warmed, with what appeared to be just some regular tabletop (not fresh-ground) black pepper shaken on top. It was served with little round toasts and a fan of thin apple slices laced with plain honey. He said it was quite good, but it wasn't as exotic as it had sounded.

My filet Rossini was fairly tender and cooked just as I had asked, and the seared foie gras was again superb, but the sauce was bland and characterless, somewhat shocking as sauces tend to be the stars of

French restaurants–they really pride themselves on this. My sides were also a letdown: "truffled" mashed potatoes were fluffy but under-seasoned, and the truffle flavor was barely detectable; a tower of limp green beans was interspersed with mushrooms whose unpleasantly slimy texture telegraphed their provenance to be a can. Marc's lobster risotto was studded with chunks of lobster meat and came with two seared scallops. Once he'd picked out all the seafood, he didn't even bother with the rest of the risotto–since he's a risotto lover, that sent a clear signal of not great.

Dessert ended the meal on a more positive note. Marc was pleased with Sophie's recommendation of L'Antillaise, a concoction made of a trio of small scoops of vanilla and coffee ice creams, toasted almonds, hot chocolate sauce, old rum and whipped cream, which she had told us was inspired by a favorite dessert she discovered in Spain, while I enjoyed a gratin of red fruits with almond sabayon and a small scoop of vanilla ice cream. Though we liked the desserts, they were not spectacular and we found them overpriced.

Overall, we wish everything had tasted as amazing as it looked. The lovely presentation made the underwhelming food a series of oddly sad surprises. Nothing was exactly terrible (except the butter), but nothing was really great (except the seared foie gras)–which is certainly not what you'd expect at one of the most expensive restaurants on the island.

Service at Spicy

We found the service excellent, though we were there on a slow night in low season, which may not be an indicator of how they do in a high-season rush. Co-owner Sophie was absolutely delightful–very warm, funny and attentive. Our waiter was also friendly, professional and solicitous. They were both knowledgeable and helpful with recommendations, and one of them was always right there just as we needed something.

Atmosphere at Spicy

Every time we'd passed outside Spicy, we sensed a quiet ambience, good for conversation, which is exactly what we found inside. It's not where you'd go for a fun night out with friends, or to get really comfortable and chill out, but it could be romantic depending on your taste–it's not cozy, but you could easily have an intimate chat.

It's notable that Spicy has the only dining room in Grand Case that's not open to the street or the beach in some way. This could be a plus or a minus, depending what you like. It allows the dining room to be air conditioned, quiet and protected, and you could watch high season's Mardi Tuesday Harmony Nights celebration from the windows without being part of the bustle. But you miss out on the French café-culture charm of Grand Case–you just don't feel as if you're dining in a small European seaside town the way you do in virtually any other restaurant in town.

Bottom Line

We wouldn't tell our friends to go to Spicy...there's no reason to pay that much for food that's just ok, especially with so much truly mind-blowing gourmet cuisine just steps away.

Le Pressoir
Overall Rating ★★☆☆☆

We visited Le Pressoir early on a Thursday night. We didn't have reservations, so we headed there at the blue-haired hour of 6 p.m. in the hopes that we'd be able to slip through and get a table.

We did get a table... but balcony was the only option. In general, I love eating outside, and in fact am a huge proponent. Seemed like a good idea at the time...

Food at Le Pressoir

The food was acceptable, but not worth the money. We ordered a bottle of Sancerre – and in fact it turned out it was the same Sancerre we had in a previous night at now-defunct Hibiscus, but for 48 euros instead of 36 euros. The bottle was not 33% larger.

I ordered the "House Speciality," which was an assortment of grilled shellfish for the first course, and grilled fish for the second course. The first course was delicious. The grilled lobster, shrimp, "flathead" lobster and scallops were perfectly cooked, and when dipped in the lemon beurre sauce, were delectable. The fish, however, was bland and only so-so. There were four kinds, each on a bed of whipped something-or-other, and nothing was really that memorable. It wasn't bad, just not worth the price of the ticket.

Steve had the lobster bisque, which he described as "as expected." The scallops with duck were delicious if you like a citron butter sauce. In his

Just the Facts

Price Level: $$$$$	*Credit Cards:* Visa
Category: French	*Currency:* market rate
Meals Served: Dinner	*Outdoor seating:* roadside balcony
Location: 30 Grand Case Boulevard	
Phone: 0590 87 76 62	*Parking:* Nearby lot

Pros

Grilled shellfish appetizer was delicious, with tasty lemon beurre sauce

Interior decor looked inviting

Cons

Bugs galore! Don't sit outside, especially near or after sunset; Food wasn't as high quality as expected for the price; Wine was particularly expensive world, the smoked mashed potatoes were a highlight.

We skipped dessert given the hordes of bugs that continued to swarm us, and headed home for a glass of port at the L'Esplanade.

Service at Le Pressoir

The waitress was professional and gave helpful advice on the food. However, when the hostess asked us how our evening was going, and we said the food was lovely but the bugs were bothering us, she replied "yes, I know, the first hour after sunset is a problem..." and shrugged and walked away. Even though there were many empty tables inside the restaurant, and they were empty well into the evening, we were never offered one. I was appalled.

Atmosphere at Le Pressoir

About 10 minutes after sitting down on the balcony, the sun went down, and the bugs came out. We've become all too familiar, in fact biblically familiar, with the tropical mosquitos. But these were a genre of bug we haven't encountered before – like flying ants, but far more insidious. And they came out in droves as the sun went down. Initially there was a lamp on our table, which thankfully the waitress turned off after the first horde arrived – on our butter, in our wine, around our water bottle. But then we realized we were sitting next to the fluorescent lights on the outside of the balcony that never get turned off.

Inside, Le Pressoir looked elegant and refined. Though it's on the sea-side of Grand Case Boulevard, it is not in fact open to the water or

Mood

Romance	★★★☆☆
Relaxation	★★☆☆☆
Fun	★★☆☆☆
Family	★☆☆☆☆
Value	★★☆☆☆

Food

Taste	★★☆☆☆
Innovation	★★★☆☆
Display	★★★★☆
Drinks	★★★☆☆

Service

Attentive	★★★☆☆
Speed	★★★★☆
Knowledge	★★★☆☆

Atmosphere

Views	★☆☆☆☆
Decor	★★★☆☆
Comfort	★☆☆☆☆
Noise	★★☆☆☆

beach. The balcony is on the road, and though it's elevated to avoid being right in the thick of traffic, it isn't particularly picturesque or pleasant.

Bottom Line

I wasn't overly impressed with Le Pressoir, especially not for the prices, though I admit I may have been too distracted by the bugs to assess fairly.

Fan Favorites - Gourmet Restaurants

Our Facebook fans love the gourmet restaurants in Grand Case. Here's what they had to say:

Sandy - Le Cottage was my favorite place also. The souffle is still being craved!!!

Shirley - have you ever eaten at Le Pressoir in Grand Case? That's where we ate the last time and it was wonderful. Service was great, food was great, wine was great!! :)

Anne Marie - La Villla opened last Oct. in Grand Case the food is terrific--- the service is great

Ann - terrific Italian restaurant in Case was Spiga...I have never tasted such delicious ravioli in my life. i'd fly there just for that alone. awesome folks. you won't be disappointed. it's more italian than italian.

Stephanie - Just came back from St. Martin...7 nights at L'Esplanade - it was wonderful!! We didn't want to leave - rooms, location and the people were fantastic. Our favorite beach was Friar's Bay, although we had a good time at the Palm Beach Bar at Orient Beach, too. Had fabulous meals in Grand Case every night... highlights were the Lolo's, Ti Provencal, Le Cottage and Spiga. Can't wait to go back.

Didi - Restaurant: for dinner, The fish pot in grand case... for breakfast, La Samanna (of course) phew, what a view!!!

Gwendolyn -Visited last week and this week. For the lolos Talk of the Town. fine dining: Le Presoir, L'Auberge Gourmade.

Suzanne - [Fish Pot] they have a lobster tank in front and it is a romantic bistro....been there several times in Grand Case also Le Cottage isnt bad either...!

Fan Favorites - Gourmet Restaurants

Beyond Grand Case, there are plenty of other fan favorites to visit:

Jo Anne - Favorite gourmet has to be La Gondola...the Osso Bucco is to die for !!! but everything is SOOO GOOD, difficult to choose

Mary - Just got back. Had a great dinner at restaurant 'L'Astrolabe' [Orient Beach], I'd recommend it. aren't too many restaurants to brag about on the Dutch side but I did find 2. First there is 'Stone' a little hideaway by the Pelican resort. Just go to their parking lot & ask the man at the gate. It is downstairs by the water, very good! Then to die for, 'Piece of Cake' on Welfare Road, 68 in Simpson Bay. A wonderful little French cafe with everything homemade, yummmm! Also 'Bliss' next to Maho Beach, a fusion type place with excellent food. The French side is expensive but worth it! The Dutch side you get what you pay for......

Arlene - Too many to choose from however one of our favorite would have to be Astrolabe an outstanding french restaurant in Orient Bay. We just came back and have eaten there many times and never been disappointed. The service is excellent, it's the restaurant to go for a romantic night out, and be sure to get the table beside the pool.

Deb - Mario's Bistro...hands down! Probably the best , not just in SXM, but the whole Caribbean!!!!

Tim - Le Taitu in Cul de Sac near the old Mont Vernon Hotel. Terrific atmosphere, combining indoor and outdoor elements. Food is the greatest and the staff always treat us like royalty. We always make it a point to have a romantic dinner on the second level there each and every trip.

Maureen - Côté Plages - Orient Beach Village is by far my favorite gourmet restaurant. Food is fabulous, service is outstanding and the Cream Brulee Trio is to die for!!

casual restaurants

casual restaurant reviews

*T*hin-crust pizzas with spicy oil, Vietnamese nems, traditional pastas, tasty salads... sometimes you don't need fancy, you just want a basic, casual meal in a mellow environment. Whether you're exhausted from a day in the sun, or looking for more reasonable prices, Grand Case's magical culinary treats aren't limited to haute cuisine.

LUCINDA'S LIST
GUIDEBOOK COMPANY

Just the Facts

Price Level:
$$$$

Category:
Steaks/Seafood

Meals Served:
Lunch, Dinner

Location:
176 Grand
Case Boulevard

Phone:
0590 87 55 80

Website:
rainbow-
cafe.com

Credit Cards:
Visa

Currency:
1 $ = 1 euro

*Outdoor
seating:* Beach
& veranda

Parking:
On site lot

Good for:
Kids, Groups

Pros

Take control of your meal: you get to mix/match meat, size, everything!

Great service, very engaging and helpful, and easy on the eyes

Beautiful beach and sunset

Cons

Random Christmas music; bugs on the veranda; not very innovative

Rainbow Cafe
Overall Rating ★★★★☆

Back in the day, Rainbow Cafe was one of the original restaurants that helped put Grand Case on the map as a culinary destination, but it closed a while ago. As of April 1st, 2010, it has been re-opened under new management. From what we have been told, the new incarnation has stayed relatively true to the original – similar menu, similar decor. We'd been hearing mixed reviews from our local friends as to the food quality, and were anxious to see whether they had worked out the kinks enough to keep the revival in business.

Food at Rainbow Cafe

My favorite thing about the Rainbow Cafe is that they put the power in your hands. Want a smaller steak? You got it. Want a leaner cut? No problem. Medium rare? You betcha. Bearnaise sauce? Bien sur. The entire menu is such that you get to choose the type of food (ribeye? filet? grouper?), the size of your meal (200g? 300g?), and then mix and match it with whatever sauce makes your heart go boom.

But first, we ordered the chicken "nems" for an appetizer. Don't know what nems are? I didn't either before lunch at Karibuni on Pinel, or Le Cottage for that matter. But apparently everyone on the island seems to have heard of nems. It's not that I've never *had* them – they're fried spring rolls, like you get from any half-decent Vietnamese or Thai restaurant. Here they're called "nems." Maybe a shortening of Vietnamese? I like to think perhaps it's because they're so yummy, you just mumble "yum, nem, yum, nem" to yourself as you eat them, kind of like Homer Simpson. Either way, the chicken nems were scrumptious at Rainbow Cafe. The dipping sauce was tasty and sweet, though I personally could have used a little more tang to it. All told, my mom and I demolished the eight pieces, despite being "not very hungry."

Our steaks arrived, complete with a handy little flag identifying their preparation. My thinly sliced 200g ribeye was perfectly medium rare. I had splurged and gone for two sauces... ok, three if you include my mom's: poivre, béarnaise and morel (mushroom). The poivre sauce had such potential, but in the end was slightly too salty. The morel sauce, even with the $5 up-charge, just wasn't that good, not sure why. Perhaps it was simply too foresty for an island meal? Oh, but the béarnaise! The béarnaise sauce was exquisite. Thick, rich, tons of tarragon, more butter and cream than a girl should eat in a month... it was delightful, and perfect for dipping, in its happy little gravy boat. Plenty for the two of us.

Mood

Romance	★★★☆☆
Relaxation	★★★★☆
Fun	★★★☆☆
Family	★★★★☆
Value	★★★☆☆

Food

Taste	★★★★☆
Innovation	★★★☆☆
Display	★★★☆☆
Drinks	★★★★☆

Service

Attentive	★★★★☆
Speed	★★★★★
Knowledge	★★★★☆

Atmosphere

Views	★★★★★
Decor	★★★★☆
Comfort	★★★★☆
Noise	★★★★☆

With every main dish you also get a side of sauteed veggies, including snap peas, green peppers, onions, mushrooms, all sorts of goodness, as well as a baked potato. Unfortunately the potato was a little over-garlicked, but not beyond salvage. They also brought a small salad before the main dish.

For dessert, we went with the special of the evening, the duo of pineapple and banana. They were

Pick and choose meat

limiting it to one per table, which I think made us want it all the more. As it turns out, it was tasty... but something was missing. It was a bowl of chunks of pineapple and banana, sauteed in a sugar sauce, which was sweet and delicious, but it really needed a counter-point: vanilla ice cream, a crepe, something. We told Douglas our assessment, and he offered to bring us any of those things, but by then we were pretty full and declined. But, he did bring us each two healthy shots of his homemade secret recipe rum concoction (I detected mango, passionfruit, and a whole lot of rum), by which point I'm not sure we remembered our names, much less that the dessert needed ice cream.

One note on the drinks. We went with the special of the evening, the mojitos, and they were well prepared – potent, but not too sweet. But it was funny, because when I ordered a second one (I know, lush, right?), I was told they might not have enough of the ingredients. If it's the special of the evening... shouldn't you have enough on hand to make more than two of them? But they were able to bring me a second one.

Oh, and they do 1 euro = 1 dollar, so all in, our tasty dinner for two, including a few drinks, was less than $100.

Service at Rainbow Cafe

The new owner, Douglas, is a charming, solicitous young guy who looks eerily like a French Orlando Bloom, which, you know, has its own perks (can't believe I didn't take a picture of him... doh!). Formerly the owner of Le String in Orient Beach, he traded it all in for Grand Case, bringing his smooth touch to the southern end of the boulevard. When we were on the fence as to whether or not to get wine, he astutely assessed the situation and recommended their evening special cocktail, a mojito. Sold.

When we first arrived, it was sunset, and there weren't that many patrons, so they took us straight to the prime seats on the veranda overlooking the beach. But after a few minutes, and sipping our drinks, we realized first that it was a little hot there, with no breeze. We asked them to turn on the overhead fans, and they immediately complied. But then the bugs became an issue... and again, no problem. They moved us straight to a table deeper inside, and bugs ceased to be an issue. Even beyond troubleshooting our obviously high maintenance issues of the evening, both the waitress and Douglas were helpful and solicitous.

Atmosphere at Rainbow Cafe

Rainbow Cafe is much nicer than your average beach bar or casual restaurant. In fact, I was hard-pressed to decide how to categorize them at first. They have fancy new red high-tech beach chairs, with built-in shades to shield your face, and huge umbrellas, on a lovely stretch of Grand Case beach with flat, clean, calm waters. For lunch, they serve a predominantly burger-based menu on the beach, and they plan to serve breakfast in the high season. And yet, they have lovely interior decor, with substantial, cushioned chairs, and generally feel like way more than a beach bar. And they serve fairly high-end fare (albeit not gourmet in my book). In the end, I decided to put these guys in the "Casual" bucket, even though their price is slightly higher than the average casual.

Oh, and did I mention their phenomenal sunset views? They have a two-tiered veranda so that everyone gets a decent look over the Caribbean. However, when we first arrived right at sunset we sat on the lower veranda, just next to the beach, and were attacked by some tiny bugs who apparently love twilight (luckily not mosquitos, or their cousins, vampires). When we moved to the upper tier they magically went away.

Of course, I would be remiss if I didn't mention that the most amusing part of the evening was the music. In general it was kind of a Rat Pack melange, with some Duke Ellington, Ella Fitzgerald and John Coltrane thrown in for good measure, which is totally appropriate. But at one point, I am not making this up, they were

Open dining room

playing Christmas music. In August. Perhaps they see this newfound lease on the Rainbow Cafe to be like a gift? Hard to say, but it was kind of comical, especially because it was on a repeated loop.

Bottom line
Rainbow Cafe doesn't compete for the gourmets, but if you're in the mood for a mellow, solid casual meal in Grand Case, set a little away from the general melee downtown, this is a good bet.

Beautiful sunset

Just the Facts

Price Level:
$$$

Category:
Pizza, Seafood

Meals Served:
Lunch,
Afternoon,
Dinner

Location:
134 Grand
Case Boulevard

Phone:
0590 87 55 57

Website:
california-
restaurant.net

Credit Cards:
Visa

Currency:
1 $ = 1 euro

Outdoor
seating: Beach
balcony

Parking:
Nearby lot

Good for:
Kids, Groups

Pros

Delicious, local French mussels
with island zest, or try their thin-
crust pizzas

Beautiful, mellow place
overlooking the beach and sunset

1 dollar = 1 euro!

Cons

Service attentiveness only so-so

La California
Overall Rating ★★★★☆

After hearing rave reviews from
other travelers for their mussels
and pizzas, we hit La California for
lunch to check what all the fuss
was about. Having spent the late
morning lounging on the beach in
front of Le Petit Hotel, we simply
walked down the beach and up
the stairs to La California's open
patio. We dipped our sandy feet
in their handy little tub of rinse
water, and sat down for a lovely
meal. Lured back with the promise
of tasty thin-crust pizzas on our
second trip, we dipped our entire
bodies in the warm Caribbean
waters before we wandered up
for a light lunch.

Food at La California
Turns out the rumors are true: La
California is the place to go for
mussels in Grand Case. Their menu
listed at least a dozen different
enticing preparations, but in the
end, I decided to go with the
traditional moules provencale.

They were excellent, as were the
requisite frites, a critical
component of French mussels in
my experience. With a light white

wine sauce, replete with garlic and other goodies, the mussels were a perfect light meal on a hot day, especially when paired with a crisp, chilled glass of sauvignon blanc.

Steve went the other route: pizza and Carib beer. When asked to describe his pizza, he replied "same." In other words, exactly up to par with the the other tasty thin-crust delicacies we had been experiencing for six weeks. Nothing to sniff at.

When my mom and I returned to partake in the thin-crust pizzas after a morning of running around the island, we were relieved to find they were just as tasty as ever. The crust is paper-thin. Ingredients fresh. Sauce piquant (hot pepper oil) added a splash of spice. My "Reine" pizza was decorated with small strips of ham, chopped mushrooms and olives. They could have left the pizza in for one more minute, just enough to brown the cheese, but then it would have risked the perfect golden doneness of the crust. My mom's "Antillaise" pizza had some of the freshest, tastiest pepperoni I've had in a long time, complete with that zing of spice.

Looking at their menu, they also have an extensive offering of crepes. I'm bummed I didn't try them while I was there – love me some crepes! – but the pizzas were so filling we couldn't eat another bite. We definitely could have split one for a light lunch. The pizzas ran around 14 euros each, and with a 1:1 euro to dollar exchange, you cannot complain.

While Steve and I were leisurely sipping our standard white wine and Carib on our first visit, we observed

Mood

Romance	★★★★☆
Relaxation	★★★★★
Fun	★★★★☆
Family	★★★★☆
Value	★★★★★

Food

Taste	★★★★☆
Innovation	★★★☆☆
Display	★★★★☆
Drinks	★★★★★

Service

Attentive	★★★☆☆
Speed	★★★★☆
Knowledge	★★★☆☆

Atmosphere

Views	★★★★★
Decor	★★★☆☆
Comfort	★★★★☆
Noise	★★★★☆

a crazy concoction of ice cream and alcohol walk by to another table. Chocolate syrup, vanilla ice cream, and obviously some tasty rum were involved. When we inquired of our waiter about this magical tasty treat, he brought us over a small glass to sample. It was the leftover bit, and I suspect he had his own eye on it, so I give him props for sharing. It was phenomenal. Not what you would go for if you wanted to get drunk – it

Restaurant - and a boutique

was as filling as an ice cream sundae – but perfect as a little dessert to finish up our meal.

Atmosphere at La California

La California is one of those fortunate Grand Case restaurants located directly above the beach. As I said, we walked straight up the beach stairs, directly onto their spacious balcony overlooking, well,

All day dining

Very few restaurants in GC are open continuously from lunch thru dinner. If you find yourself on the beach, having snoozed right thru the lunch hour, La California is your place for a mid-afternoon pick-me-up.

everything. They don't bother with windows or doors, just put up a railing and a roof to provide some shade, and Bob's your uncle. The wicker chairs may not look comfortable, but they were actually OK.

Though La California didn't actually remind me of California – I'm unclear as to why that is the name, and the irony is that they write "French and Italian Cuisine" directly on the sign – it was certainly a perfect example of island decor. Bright red, with zen accents. Embrace the beauty all around you, and the colors of the tropics, and you can't go wrong. At least not too wrong.

When my mom and I went there for a pre-dinner drink one evening, we were fortunate to get there right at golden hour, as the sun was preparing to set. Leisurely sipping our sauvignon blanc, we were able to capture stunning sunset photos as some kids eked out the last of the daylight frolicking on the beach. Spectacular. So if you arrive early in Grand Case for your gourmet meal, stop by La California to get your aperitif and sunset fix.

They've also got free Wifi, and a cute little Zen boutique shop.

Service at La California

As I mentioned, I give the waiter major props for bringing us the ice cream cocktail leftovers. Tasty. Definitely got him a big tip. Beyond that, the service was fine, nothing more, nothing less. They didn't neglect us per se, but we had more than enough time to casually linger with our drinks, watching the shadows get long on the beach. We haven't been there when it's been crowded, but during a slow time, they were similarly paced. I will say during prime lunch time, they were speedier and more on the ball.

When we had our aperitif, they were kind enough to provide "Off" spray to my mom who hadn't yet grown accustomed to dousing herself before every outing... a necessity I recommend regardless of your destination, especially if you are like my mom, a particularly tasty morsel for the Industrial Strength Mosquitos.

Bottom Line

Casual aperitif or dinner watching the sunset... mid-afternoon snacks... delicious mussels... or just

Don't forget the bug spray

craving those tasty thin-crust pizzas, La California is a great bet. I have already made plans to try those ice cream drink concoctions on my next trip, along with their extensive crepe menu.

Try the hot oil on the pizzas

Just the Facts

Price Level:
$$

Category:
Steaks, Seafood

Meals Served:
Dinner

Location:
Rue des Ecoles

Phone:
0590 87 03 74

Credit Cards:
None

Currency:
market rate

*Outdoor
seating:*
Garden

Parking:
Nearby lot

Good for:
Guys, Groups

Pros

Well-prepared steak and grilled fish, with amazing creme fraiche and chive baked potatoes

Where else can you be a pirate for a night? Unique, fun atmosphere with Marcel, your authentic pirate

Cons

Bathroom is x-rated; wooden benches are a little hard

Pirate Grill
Overall Rating ★★★★☆

You don't go to the Pirate Grill for the food, although it is surprisingly good. You go to have the kind of experience that is, frankly, outside that of most Americans.   OK, maybe not just "outside"... more like the French outre.

Marcel, the Pirate Captain himself, is 70 if he's a day, and has lived in St. Martin for 27 years. Up until 1995, he sailed his pirate ship in and around Grand Case, and shared the pirate's life with tourists... until Hurricane Luis decimated his floating home and livelihood. But, being an enterprising sort, and a carpenter to boot, Marcel recovered what he could and rebuilt his pirate ship on land as Repaire de Pirate (the Pirate Grill), just off the Grand Case Boulevard, across from Crousti Boulangerie (yes, that's really the name). Marcel is a charming pirate, always in costume and character, complete with bare feet, pirate hat and pirate shirt (Seinfeld would be proud). The restaurant is only open Thurs, Fri & Sat in the low season (more in the high season)... but even then, no guarantees, because who knows when a pirate might need to be off sacking a galleon?

When we arrived at the Pirate Grill, I was sure we were in the right place... and yet the door was locked. We peered through the slats at the windows, and could see our friends seated at the bar. So I rang the ship's bell. A portal opened up, a bright blue eye in a salty grizzled face peered through, and then an ancient pistol emerged accompanied by an authentic "Aargh, matey!" It was brilliant. Eventually he let us in to his pirate den.

Food at the Pirate Grill

The Pirate Grill doesn't have a printed menu. In true French form, the day's menu is spelled out on a portable chalkboard, one side in French and the other in English (somehow the English side is much sparser, even though the same dishes are served regardless of nationality as far as we could tell). In true pirate form, the menu is in general limited to what you imagine a bachelor pirate would be able to whip up on a boat: grilled steak, grilled fish, kabobs of grilled steak or fish.

I experienced a little trepidation at ordering wine in what felt like more of a bar than a restaurant (this was before I tasted the tastiness), but as my friends reminded me, he's French, so of course he has a couple decent bottles of Cotes du Rhone and Bordeaux.

Mood

Romance	★★★☆☆
Relaxation	★★★☆☆
Fun	★★★★★
Family	★★★☆☆
Value	★★★★★

Food

Taste	★★★★☆
Innovation	★★★☆☆
Display	★★★★☆
Drinks .	★★★★★

Service

Attentive	★★★★☆
Speed	★★★☆☆
Knowledge	★★★★☆

Atmosphere

Views	★☆☆☆☆
Decor	★★★★★
Comfort	★★★☆☆
Noise	★★★★☆

But don't let the limited menu fool you. There were five of us enjoying our post-pillaging pirate repast, and every dish was perfectly prepared. When our English divemaster friend was asked to describe his Assiette de Boucanier (Buccaneer's Plate) of assorted grilled goodies, he expounded: "This is the dog's bollocks. The small faux filet was perfectly steaky, the grouper was juicy and meaty, the shrimp was

Grilled faux filet

According to Madam J: "the flavorful flank steak seemed to be marinated with garlic and fresh herbs...and it hit the spot excellently. The au poivre sauce was expertly balanced, the peppercorns were there with a bite to punctuate the buttery creaminess, but did not overwhelm it with too peppery firepower."

So the steaks, the kabobs and the grilled fish all represented well... but we all agreed the true highlight was the baked potato. Every dish came with a baked potato, and though it was properly prepared in and of itself, not too dry or overcooked, its chief role was to act as delivery device for a generous concoction of fabulous creme fraiche and chives. I found myself accidentally eating tin foil because I couldn't stop mining for morsels.

nicely grilled–simple but pretty spot on. This is proper pirate grub."

Madam J and myself both ordered the faux filet, saignant (medium rare). Mine was perfectly cooked; after the first bite I thought to myself that it would benefit from a poivre sauce, et voila! It appeared.

In true bachelor cuisine fashion, each dish also arrived with a bit of a

Death digestif

green salad, consisting of chopped lettuce and a couple tomato slices, smothered in dressing to the point where its greenness was well enough camouflaged to be consumed.

Desserts were another surprise. The molten chocolate lava cake with vanilla ice cream and whipped cream, wow, yummy, almost caused a mutiny. Same for the bananas flambe.

At the end of the repast, when Grand Case restaurants bring out the bottles of homemade rum digestif, Marcel again doesn't disappoint. True to form, the digestif arrives in a pirate-style old tin coffeepot, complete with a skull and crossbones and "mort" etched on the side. You think you're going to have to hold your nose and take the shot, but in fact, it's utterly sippable. He told us the ingredients – rum, brandy, cognac, lemon, sugarcane, cassis and cinnamon, and oh, the cinnamon is definitely the key. He left the "bottle" and we tucked in for a few rounds.

All told, for such an elaborate and satisfying meal, it came out to $50 per person, which is a downright steal in this neck of the woods when it included a couple bottles of wine and some lethal planters' punches.

Service at the Pirate Grill

During high season Marcel has a wait staff, but seeing as how it was low season, Marcel was the man about town while his chef slaved in the open kitchen. There was only one other table of patrons, and they were seated next to us, probably to cut down on the

Secret pirate dive squirrels

amount Marcel had to travel. It added to the festive atmosphere. Marcel introduced us to the cook as he prepared to depart, so we sent him off with a well-earned round of applause.

Marcel himself is beyond charming and utterly adorable (apparently VERY lovable judging by his bathroom decor, but we'll get to that in a moment). This is one place where French is going to be very handy. I think Marcel speaks English

Flying the pirate flag

Pirate ship decorations

a Spanish galleon, with the flickering candlelit skulls and the thick wooden tables and benches which felt like they were crafted from shipwrecked timbers." It's possible the benches really were crafted from his shipwreck.

Marcel definitely put a great deal of thought and effort into replicating a true pirate experience, complete with a ceiling like that on a sailboat, and a large sail announcing the main entrance. Since we visited during low season, the outdoor patio wasn't open, but we have been told that though it's small, it's a charming spot for drinks during high season (no dinner), and frequently features a DJ, and sometimes, if you're very, very lucky, a costume dance party.

In many ways, you really are having dinner in Marcel's pirate home... literally. He lives in the back room. His adorable little old dog keeps an eye on things when she's not snoring in the corner. The kitty lounges on the window pane. And, if he likes you, Marcel might let you know that you are welcome to make yourself at home in his establishment and partake of your vices.

somewhat, but since we spoke French (more or less), it obviously endeared us to him. He does get more and more chatty as the evening wears on.

Atmosphere at the Pirate Grill

Well... where to begin. For so many restaurants in Grand Case, the atmosphere is all about the views of the sun setting over the azure waves, or whether the chairs are comfortable. The Pirate Grill is so much more interesting!

Madam J summed it up best: "I felt like we were celebrating in a secret pirate den after successfully sacking

Now, things get really interesting if you decide to visit the bathroom... the X-rated bathroom. It would seem that Marcel is a naturalist, and a bit of an exhibitionist, because the bathroom is liberally decorated with semi-pornographic (ok, maybe more than semi) photos of his close friends, with their skimpy undergarment souvenirs pinned to the wall. There is a little doorway at eye level that says "if you want a peep, ask Marcel for the key – $1."

X-Rated Warning

The dining room and patio of Pirate Grill are great fun, decked out in pirate paraphernalia. Great for kids... as long as you don't let them go into the bathroom where there are souvenirs...

There are many handwritten notes from women, many in French, and I think they may be exhorting you to go ahead and leave a little something behind when you go.

So... though this place seems like a great destination with the family – the kids will get a definite kick out of the dining room – make sure they've all used the bathroom *before* you go to dinner.

Bottom Line

If you can get past the adult-themed pirate experience in the bathroom (or maybe because you want to check it out), the Pirate Grill has a unique ambiance and satisfying culinary experience that you are unlikely to experience anywhere else. Definitely a one-of-a-kind place, and worth a visit.

Marcel, the original pirate

Just the Facts

Price Level:
$$$

Category:
Everything

Meals Served:
Lunch,
Afternoon,
Dinner

Location:
Orient Bay

Phone:
0590 51 12 12

Website:
elranchodelsol.
com

Credit Cards:
Visa

Currency:
1.2 $ = 1 euro

*Outdoor
seating:* Hilltop
picnic

Parking:
On site

Good for:
Kids, Groups

Pros

DELIVERY. Seriously. Free.

Tasty, thin-crust pizzas

Beautiful views, mellow
atmosphere on top of the hill
overlooking Orient Bay

Cons

Quality food, but nothing extra
special about it; Not walkable

Rancho Del Sol
Overall Rating ★★★★☆

When we were too tired to venture out of the hotel for dinner, or even to the grocery store to pick up supplies... it was time to call Rancho del Sol. As one of two pizza delivery options in Grand Case ("livraison" en francais), they quickly became a favorite. They bring hot, fresh, tasty thin-crust pizzas direct to your hotel door in less than half an hour. Like Domino's... only DELICIOUS. The one problem is they are closed on Saturday nights, and for some reason, this was a common hangover day for us.

Food at Rancho del Sol

Did I mention they DELIVER? One of the few restaurants that we found who did, at least on the French side, and this endeared them to us forever.

Rancho del Sol's menu is extensive, and caters to a variety of palates. They offer everything. From pizzas (definitely a highlight) to salads (also proven tasty), to huge steaks and burgers, and dare I say it, I think they even have some Mexican food, like quesadillas. An impressive menu, especially for a place that delivers. The Western and rodeo pizzas are our favorites, though we haven't sampled all of them by any stretch.

My mom and I finally crashed at the very end of our whirlwind restaurant sampling and decided to order in for our last Grand Case meal. Rancho del Sol was our go-to choice, and an awesome choice it was.

Within a very short time we were chowing down (funny how the aroma of good food revives even the tiredest of travelers) on crunchy pork nems (i.e., spring rolls) and crispy pizza, both of which arrived hot and tasty, having survived their trek.

I did have to repress my Berkeley-ingrained horror at the styrofoam container for the nems, but I was too hungry to object. The food lived up to its reputation, and we were happily replete with very little physical effort on our part. And isn't that the point of food delivery?

Atmosphere at Rancho del Sol

On the main road, north of Orient Beach, before you hit Anse Marcel or Grand Case, you will find the Rancho Del Sol restaurant. You may have already eaten there several times before you make it to their actual restaurant, and that's OK. You aren't missing out if you have them deliver, though they do have some beautiful hilltop views of Orient Bay.

The one time we stopped by Rancho del Sol to actually eat there (after all, we figured we had to see

Mood

Romance	★★★☆☆
Relaxation	★★★★☆
Fun	★★☆☆☆
Family	★★★★☆
Value	★★★☆☆

Food

Taste	★★★☆☆
Innovation	★★☆☆☆
Display	★★☆☆☆
Drinks	★★☆☆☆

Service

Attentive	★★★☆☆
Speed	★★★★★
Knowledge	★★☆☆☆

Atmosphere

Views	★★★★☆
Decor	★★☆☆☆
Comfort	★★★☆☆
Noise	★★★☆☆

where our food was coming from), we had a lovely late afternoon snack. It was relatively quiet in the

Delivery!

Rancho Del Sol gives great delivery, just remember they aren't open on Saturdays.

Tasty nems

a great place to bring the kids, given the extensive menu options, and the casualness of the dining room.

When my mom and I attempted to return during our trip, just after perusing the Marigot market, we were stymied by their odd choice to be closed on Saturdays.

Service at Rancho del Sol

These guys give great delivery – we never had to wait more than a half hour, and this was during high season. As I said, my only complaint is they aren't open on Saturdays. When we ate on site, the service was fine, though typically French in their unobtrusiveness. If we had been in a hurry, we might have had complaints... but it was mid-afternoon, and we were on island time, so who cared?

When we decided to while away the afternoon outside, taking pics of the humming birds and sipping our sauvignon blanc, they didn't bat an eye.

Bottom line

After an exhausting day at the beach, when everyone is feeling crispy and the kids are imploding (or your husband), there's nothing like fresh, fast delivery from Rancho Del Sol. Comfort food at your hotel door. Brilliant.

unassuming dining room, with almost 360-degree views up on the hill above Orient Bay.

Outside, we lingered at the outdoor couch, attempting to photograph the hummingbirds and panoramic view while we sipped our second glass of wine. Not a care in the world. This seemed like

Views of Orient Bay

Piazza Pascal
Overall Rating ★★★☆☆

Tucked away in the Petit Shops in the center of Grand Case, Piazza Pascal is a relatively new, casual Italian restaurant. It has a small but charming open-air seating area on the second floor that allows you to observe the sunset over the bay, even though you're not on the water side of the street.

Food at Piazza Pascal
First let me say this: though the name is Piazza Pascal, which conjured in my mind the anticipation of pizza, there is no pizza. I had geared myself up for a thin-crust French pizza, one of my favorite all-time meals, just assuming that it was all in the name, and hey, close enough. But there is no pizza to be had, so I had to re-calibrate my appetite.

What you do find are some delectable pasta dishes. I decided to console myself with my favorite tagliatelle carbonara... except it was linguine carbonara. Though I was slightly skeptical of the pasta switcheroo, my desire for pancetta and cream sauce overcame any trepidation. I mean, my mouth was already watering reading the description. My mom decided to go with the chicken fettucini, hoping for something basic to counteract all the rich food we've been eating every breakfast, lunch and dinner on our whirlwind research trip.

While we awaited our dinners, we ordered a wonderful bottle of Pinot Bianco white wine from Alois Legeder. It was crisp, bright and refreshing on a warm tropical evening, and a great value for $29.

The food arrived promptly, fresh and steaming hot from the kitchen. I mixed in the requisite raw egg into the carbonara sauce... only it didn't quite combine properly. I think the linguine is an unfortunate substitution for tagliatelle. Not that it

Just the Facts

Price Level: $$	Credit Cards: Visa
Category: Italian	Currency: market rate
Meals Served: Dinner	Outdoor seating: 2nd floor balcony
Location: 101 Grand Case Boulevard	Parking: Nearby lot
Phone: 0590 87 39 21	Good for: Kids, Groups
Website: piazzapascal.com	

Pros

Solid, tasty pasta dishes, served promptly and steaming hot

Fabulous service - this is a great place if you want an American-paced meal

Lovely upstairs balcony

Cons

Food is a solid B; if you have cat allergies, sit downstairs

was bad, not by any stretch, but the density of the linguine meant the pasta and cream clumped a little more than necessary. The taste was still delicious – high quality pancetta, in thinly sliced bits instead of chunks, mixed with loads of butter and cream, you couldn't really go wrong. But not as good as a tagliatelle.

My mom's chicken alfredo was filling, with a substantial portion of sliced, grilled chicken on top. Though the chicken was slightly dry, overall the effect wasn't displeasing. Her first description was that it was good, albeit fairly "Americanized." It was a solid B.

Presentation-wise, both pastas looked nice, but were somewhat lacking in the garnish department. We would have preferred less substantial portions, balanced with something green.

The highlight was definitely dessert. Despite having scarfed down copious amounts of pasta, we were lured in by the description of the bread pudding. Two slices, steeped for days in some magic nectar, sprinkled with raisins and offset by high quality vanilla ice cream, all doused with a healthy drizzle of chocolate sauce... it was heavenly. Since there didn't seem to be a complimentary house rum digestif on offer, we went crazy and ordered the homemade limoncello. Definitely another highlight. It was light and flavorful, with just enough kick to offset the sweet dessert.

Service at Piazza Pascal

The owners of Piazza Pascal are a husband and wife duo, Pascal and Donna. Pascal is French and handily presides over the kitchen, while Donna is American, and handles the front of the house with verve and style. She was engaging and extremely on the ball, never letting us feel neglected, while still leaving us alone to linger over our meal. The pace of the meal is more "American," meaning the food comes out promptly and steaming hot. Donna steered us very well in the wine department, as well as the limoncello and dessert. Pascal also came out to check on us during our meal, a nice touch.

Atmosphere at Piazza Pascal

We were fortunate to commandeer one of the three tables located on the second-floor veranda of Piazza Pascal. Removed from the Boulevard, with a peekaboo view over the tops of the restaurants across the street, it was a perfectly quiet, out of the way spot, with a delicate evening breeze to keep us cool. The decor wasn't anything noteworthy, nor objectionable. The chairs and table were comfortable enough, though nothing special. Downstairs, there were a few tables, and plenty of room for a group of eight that was eating together.

During our dinner, we noticed that there is a quiet interloper who likes to preside over the meal – a cute little gray cat who has decided the patio is part of her domain. She was never bothersome, but noteworthy if you have an allergy or strong feline objection. If you're missing your own pet, perhaps a bonus?

Bottom Line

Mood

Romance	★★☆☆☆
Relaxation	★★★☆☆
Fun	★★☆☆☆
Family	★★★☆☆
Value	★★★★☆

Food

Taste	★★★☆☆
Innovation	★★★☆☆
Display	★★☆☆☆
Drinks	★★★☆☆

Service

Attentive	★★★★☆
Speed	★★★★★
Knowledge	★★★★☆

Atmosphere

Views	★★★☆☆
Decor	★★★☆☆
Comfort	★★★☆☆
Noise	★★★★☆

Piazza Pascal is a perfect destination if you're looking for a reasonably-priced, comforting pasta meal in a quiet, intimate setting, particularly if you want a faster paced meal. Don't miss the limoncello and bread pudding for dessert.

Brasserie Des Iles
Overall Rating ★★★☆☆

Brasserie Des Iles is one of the less assuming restaurants on Grand Case Boulevard. It is a quiet, open restaurant on the "wrong" side of the street. All told, there isn't anything wildly exciting about this restaurant, except that it is a solid meal for a reasonable price, in a non-wild environment. As a result, it quickly became our standard default for those evenings when we were too hungover to go out big, and/or too tired from the sun to cook. Special note: we often ran into the local gendarmes eating here. Perhaps that is why it is so mellow and quiet? So be on your best behavior. Even when my Mom and I visited for lunch during the low season, the gendarmes were there in quiet force, along with a bunch of guys from what appeared to be a rugby league. This is a guy-friendly kind of place.

Food at Brasserie Des Iles

Menu-wise, Brasserie Des Iles offers a variety of options. Our favorite by far was the list of traditional, authentic French pizzas — particularly La Reine. If you've never had a proper French pizza,

Price Level:
$$$

Credit Cards:
Visa

Category:
Pasta, etc.

Currency:
market rate

Meals Served:
Lunch, Dinner

Outdoor seating: none

Location:
49 Grand Case Boulevard

Parking:
Nearby lot

Phone:
0590 87 87 46

Good for:
Kids, Guys, Groups

Pros

Tasty, thin-crust pizzas, and decent tagliatelle carbonara pasta

I scream, you scream, we all scream for GELATO

Mellow, quiet atmosphere for a casual night out

Cons

Nothing particularly exotic or special, this is your basic, casual restaurant try one – and don't plan to share it. With its delectable thin crust, you will easily inhale the entire thing before you realize what's happening. Try the spicy oil. Trust me. (But start slow, if you're not used to spicy). They have decent salads, including a salade de pays (country salad) that is very hearty. My mom and I both had salads the day we visited: Mom's tomato-mozzarella salad (13 euros) was beautifully presented and quite delicious as well as being a substantial size; my shrimp and avocado salad (also 13 euros, the pricing is a bit of a mystery) contained a large half avocado on a bed of baby lettuce, and was filled to overflowing with shrimp and crab dressed with a nicely seasoned mayonnaise. Accompanied by the inevitable basket of baguette slices, the salads made a satisfying "ladies lunch" in the midst of all that testosterone, although the salads were also being eaten with apparent gusto by members of the rugby team.

One night I went crazy and ordered the tagliatelle pasta. This was difficult for me, because when I studied in France oh, what, 20 years ago (eek!), it was one of my absolute favorite dishes. With its heavy cream sauce, chunks of pancetta (mmm, bacon) and topped off with a raw egg in the middle, it's not what you'd call health-conscious, or even FDA-approved. I've never found it properly made in the States, and have always been disappointed. But Brasserie des Iles did not disappoint. I wouldn't say it was the best I've ever had, but it certainly did the trick. My dazed food coma

Mood	
Romance	★★☆☆☆
Relaxation	★★★☆☆
Fun	★★★☆☆
Family	★★★★☆
Value	★★★★☆

Food	
Taste	★★★☆☆
Innovation	★★☆☆☆
Display	★★★☆☆
Drinks	★★★☆☆

Service	
Attentive	★★☆☆☆
Speed	★★★☆☆
Knowledge	★★★☆☆

Atmosphere	
Views	★☆☆☆☆
Decor	★★★☆☆
Comfort	★★★☆☆
Noise	★★★☆☆

was so good Steve had to roll me back up the hill.

Most importantly, Brasserie des Iles also serves yummy gelato, both in the dining room and on the street. Delicious on a warm Caribbean evening, or as a delectable finish to the "ladies lunch."

Shrimp and crab salad

Service at Brasserie des Iles

What to say about the service? It's fine. Nothing commendable, nothing reprehensible. I give it the old Gallic shrug. They aren't that quick on bringing out rounds of drinks, but that might have just

Open dining room

been because they were busy over-serving the gendarmes, and who can blame them? The service was similar for my mom's and my lunch during the slow season. The waitress let us experiment with our French, and was quite patient, which helped make up for the casual neglect.

Atmosphere at Brasserie des Iles

Though the Brasserie isn't on the ocean, it is wide open to the night breeze. The chairs aren't the most comfortable – your basic wooden sort, minimal cushion – but this isn't a restaurant where you're going to spend three hours at dinner. It's a quaint, convivial atmosphere overall; we often chatted with other couples at nearby tables. The decor is uniquely French island, with wooden fish and an heirloom map of the Caribbean sea.

Bottom Line

Even with the tables of eight gendarmes toward the back, it was never loud or obnoxious... just mellow. Exactly what you need after a long day in the sun, or if you're trying to rush back to the hotel to catch American Idol on a Wednesday night.

Il Nettuno
Overall Rating ★★★☆☆

Reviewed by Vicki, Lucinda's mom, a.k.a. "Grey Squirrel"

Granted, we went to Il Nettuno when we were dog-tired from spending a wonderful day at Pinel. And granted, both of us come from cities where great gourmet Italian food is easily available, so maybe we're jaded and fussy. Within that frame of reference, Il Nettuno is just OK. It's one of the larger restaurants on Grand Case's Restaurant Row and has a beautiful view of the bay, but the food, well, it's just sufficient.

Food at Il Nettuno
After being greeted by one of the charming owners and passing by the shrine to the Washington Redskins (the owner spent time in McLean, Virginia), we were seated and almost immediately given some bruschetta to whet our appetite, along with a menu.

Ah, the menu... Heavy on veal and chicken pasta dishes, standard marsala, saltimbocca and piccata, no pizza (at least at dinner). Both pastas and desserts are home-made. Actually, home-made is a good description of the food in general: this is the food that your Italian Nonna would prepare for family gatherings at her home near the Jersey Shore, i.e., generous servings of solid, carb-heavy nutrition.

Entrees, priced in euros, run from about 18 to 28. There is a small, but adequate wine list, and wines are available by the glass. Two pasta entrees, a shared dessert, a bottle of water, and two glasses of wine came to $90, typical of the casual non-lolo Grand Case restaurants.

Tagliatelle w/ chicken & spinach

Just the Facts

Price Level: $$$	Credit Cards: Visa, Amex
Category: Italian	Currency: market rate
Meals Served: Dinner	Outdoor seating: overlooking beach
Location: 70 Grand Case Boulevard	
	Parking: Nearby lot
Phone: 0590 87 77 38	Good for: Kids, Groups
Website: ilnettuno.com	

Pros

On the water, with several tables overlooking the sunset

Decent, filling italian food, generous portions and served hot and fresh

Cons

Food and ambience unmemorable - relying on their water views to carry the day

Beware the wandering minstrel

My tagliatelle with spinach and chicken was not too oily and not too heavily spiced: good, but not spectacular. The same verdict applied to the chicken marsala with spaghetti enjoyed by my daughter. The lemon torta we tried was acceptable, if a little too sweet and heavy on the crust component.

If you were traveling with children, Il Nettuno would be an especially good dining option, although we saw no children while we were there. A number of couples seemed to be enjoying romantic dinners at tables just overlooking the beach, although the lighting was more senior-friendly than seductive.

Service at Il Nettuno

The service was casual, but politely attentive. We were probably too tired to attempt much interaction; but didn't feel that the wait staff encouraged camaraderie with the guests, at least not to the degree that most Grand Case restaurants do. They didn't provide much in the way of direction or recommendations. The restaurant was not crowded when we were there, and the good news is they brought the food out relatively fast, and it was hot, straight from the pot.

Atmosphere at Il Nettuno

The decor is reminiscent of some restaurants I went to years ago in Atlantic City: sentimentally over-decorated, although with enough airy Island vibe mixed in to make it pleasant enough. There is a huge mirror on one wall, reflecting the view, but kind of cheesy.

Though the sound of the water lapping underneath the balcony is pleasant, they have a large fountain for the lobster that makes a loud splashing noise, competing with the noise of the Caribbean, which seemed like a waste to me. The chairs are of the bad wedding variety, and didn't really encourage you to want to linger.

When Lucinda visited Il Nettuno during high season, she was fairly horrified to find they had roaming musicians going around to the tables; she and her husband made it clear they weren't interested in that brand of "romance," and they weren't bothered again.

Bottom line

Il Nettuno is the sort of restaurant for a reliably adequate meal in pleasant surroundings, especially when you don't feel up to a three-hour event, but it's not a gourmet destination. Though it has beautiful views overlooking the beach and sunset, it lacks the intimate feel of other Grand Case restaurants. Makes sense more for a large family outing than a romantic evening.

Mood

Romance	★★☆☆☆
Relaxation	★★★☆☆
Fun	★★☆☆☆
Family	★★★☆☆
Value	★★☆☆☆

Food

Taste	★★★☆☆
Innovation	★★☆☆☆
Display	★★★☆☆
Drinks	★★☆☆☆

Service

Attentive	★★★☆☆
Speed	★★★★☆
Knowledge	★★☆☆☆

Atmosphere

Views	★★★★★
Decor	★★☆☆☆
Comfort	★★☆☆☆
Noise	★★★☆☆

Le Soleil
Overall Rating ★★☆☆☆

Just the Facts

Price Level:
$$$$

Category:
Alsatian

Meals Served:
Lunch, Dinner

Location:
60 Grand Case
Boulevard

Phone:
0590 87 92 32

Credit Cards:
Visa

Currency:
market rate

Outdoor seating:
overlooking beach

Parking:
Nearby lot

Pros

Simple atmosphere, with good views of the beach and Caribbean

Steve's shrimp with coconut sauce did have redeeming value, as did the Alsatian Tarte Flambee

Cons

Terrible tuna steak, had to send it back it was so fishy; Gazpacho was terrible; Abysmal service

My husband and I went to Le Soleil the day after we first arrived in Grand Case. Instead of asking for a recommendation from someone knowledgeable, we decided to wander the Boulevard until we saw a place that spoke to us. We picked Le Soleil because it seemed less fancy than the rest, but still French. We hadn't yet adjusted to the extra hour time difference, so we were too early to realize that the restaurant was emptier than the rest. We missed the warning signs. Even when my mom and I returned during low season to give it another shot... sad to say, it still fell short.

Food at Le Soleil

Steve ordered reasonably well – he got the shrimp and pineapple kebob with curry sauce, which was actually fairly tasty, kind of sweet and spicy at the same time (though we've had better since). I, unfortunately, did not do as well. I ordered a tuna steak, which seemed like a good idea – we were, after all, in the Caribbean, next to the Sea. But it was awful. The tuna was fishy. It tasted completely off. I hate sending food back, but in this case, I had to. I risked food poisoning, and though I tried a couple bites, it simply wasn't edible.

When my mom and I returned to Grand Case in August, we decided to give Le Soleil another shot, at least for lunch. Perhaps we had hit it on an off day? After all, my husband's dish was decent. So we went. I ordered an Alsatian "Tarte Flambee Gratinee." It sounded like a quiche-like dish, with creme fraiche, bacon, onions and swiss cheese. Even if it wasn't a quiche, I figured you can't go too wrong with those ingredients. It was a hot day, and tomato season, so my mom ordered the gazpacho. We got some fries as well, just in case.

As it turns out, the Alsatian Tarte Flambees are more like ultra thin-crust pizza, only with creme fraiche instead of marinara sauce. It was, in fact, fairly tasty, even if it wasn't what I expected. The creme fraiche definitely makes it richer than your average lunch. My mom's gazpacho, on the other hand... not so much. Though it was presented well, with cucumber slices and parsley adorning the bowl, it was so overly inundated with garlic that it wasn't edible - and I'm a huge fan of garlic, so I don't say that lightly. Also, they had some tomato slices as garnish, which were so barely red that they bore no resemblance to anything you'd consider ripe. In my book, you can't even begin to consider making gazpacho if you start with bad tomatoes; the whole endeavor was doomed from the outset. Luckily we had the tarte and the frites to get us through, so at least we didn't starve.

Mood

Romance	★★☆☆☆
Relaxation	★★☆☆☆
Fun	★★☆☆☆
Family	★★☆☆☆
Value	★☆☆☆☆

Food

Taste	★★☆☆☆
Innovation	★★☆☆☆
Display	★★☆☆☆
Drinks	★★☆☆☆

Service

Attentive	★☆☆☆☆
Speed	★☆☆☆☆
Knowledge	★☆☆☆☆

Atmosphere

Views	★★★★★
Decor	★★☆☆☆
Comfort	★★☆☆☆
Noise	★★★☆☆

So there you have it. For the record, not ALL restaurants in Grand Case are incredible. After two tries, we had only 50-50 luck each time, which as they say is great for baseball, but that's about it. Saddest part is that it wasn't even inexpensive – our light lunch ran about $50 - and they still charged me for a meal that first visit when I had to send back the tuna.

Lovely views and ambiance

Service at Le Soleil

We were the only people in the restaurant for at least the first half of our first dinner. And yet... the service was terrible. When I realized my tuna was inedible, it took 15 minutes to get the waitress' attention to ask her to take it back. She didn't even apologize. She looked suspicious, and only grudgingly offered to bring me something else, as though cooking the tuna further would improve it. I ordered what Steve had. It was another 20 minutes or so before my food arrived, long after he was done his meal.

During our lunch, the waitress (same one as last time) was slightly better, at least she didn't completely ignore us. But have you ever noticed that sometimes, when a waitress checks in on you, they don't actually want an honest answer? I definitely got the sense she didn't care whether we were in fact enjoying our meal, only that there wasn't some horrific complaint, and even then, I was

unconvinced. Perhaps I'm not being fair, but I definitely didn't get the warm and fuzzies. All told, I was unimpressed with the attitude or quality of the service at Le Soleil.

Atmosphere at Le Soleil

It's too bad the food and service are so unfortunate, because the atmosphere is lovely. There isn't much decor to speak of, but they don't need it – they are on the "good" side of Grand Case Boulevard, blessed with an open-air balcony overlooking the beach and clear Caribbean sea. It was a pretty, casual atmosphere, which we would have been happy to return to, had it not been for the poor quality food and service. There are only a handful of tables, so it's quiet and relaxing. The deck juts out a little further than it's neighbors, so it's well positioned to catch more of the sea breezes, and it was in fact pleasant even during the heat of the day.

Bottom Line

After two attempts at Le Soleil, we were simply unimpressed by the quality of food and service. There are definitely better places to try in Grand Case.

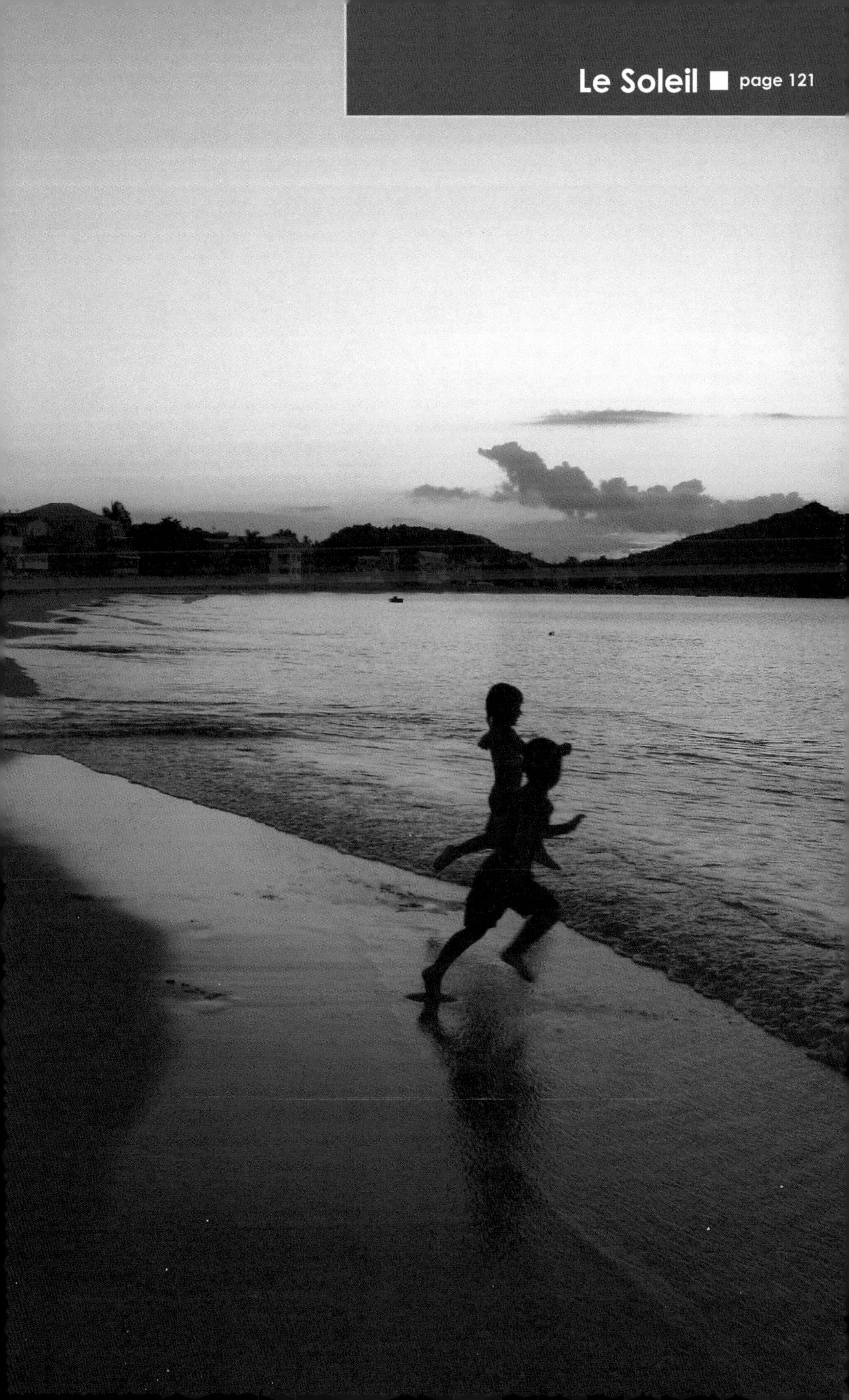

Fan Favorites - Casual Restaurants

Our Facebook fans have their favorite casual restaurants too. Here's what they have to say about the ones in Grand Case:

Beth - Rainbow Cafe is definitely one of my favorite places to visit on the island. The owners are very friendly and the staff are attentive and accommodating. Every time I visit, they make me feel like family. The owner, Douglas, looks like a French Orlando Bloom. The food is also amazing. I love the salmon dishes. Rainbow Cafe is a must visit for St. Martin.

Angie - aaah, but their pizza is the best!! we LOVE La California..we vacation in Grand Case every year, we rent an apartment over La California overlooking beautiful Grand Case Beach, and we love the restaurant! Delicious food, many choices on the menu, beautiful view, very friendly staff.

Vicky -We had a wonderful experience last year at La California! I had the salmon pizza and it was absolutely delicious!! I remember our friends had salads that were wonderful too! Like you...we were way too full to try the delicious crepes...but I am planning on trying them when we return in the spring! Can't wait! :-)

Mary Grace - The Pirate in Grand Case is our favorite restaurant!! Marcelle is a wonderful host, and the food is ALWAYS delicious! For a memorable meal, head to the Pirate!

Tim -We had lunch at the Pirate Grill one day. The staff was very cheerful and accommodating, saying my wife could eat in the nude if she wanted to (she didn't). Had a great fish sandwich and a great time there. Will probably stop in there again this Dec.

Jennifer - Very much agree with your mother's assessment of Il Nettuno. Good, not great, food. Great view. High prices. Matteo, the wandering minstrel...yikes!

Fan Favorites - Casual Restaurants

Beyond Grand Case, here are other fan favorites for casual dining:

Ann - La Belle Epoch in the Marina in Marigot. Thin-crust pizza, caesar salad, bottle of Cote de Rhone.

Karen - Busby's Bar, which is located on Dawn Beach right in the sand. A gorgeous setting for lunch and great food!!!

Paula Jean - there is one other place that has the most unbelievable food: Loterie Farm. Coming from New England, I would say their fish and chips would put any thing here to shame. Their iced tea is yummy. The swinging from the tree is not for the faint at heart, but well worth the ride. If you keep on driving past Loterie, you will reach the highest point on St. Maartin. It is amazing!

Karen - check out Zee Best, a wonderful breakfast spot with homemade crepes and omelets, the Greenhouse near the boardwalk is a great lunch spot , the sister restaurant by the water check out the fri. nite lobster nite if available,

Jeanne - I will be coming back to the island early April. It will be my 12th trip. I love Le Tropicana, Le Petit Auburge at the marina in Marigot and Saratoga by Simpson Bay Pharmacy.

Karen - We have always loved La Rosa 11 over by Maho & Cheri's. Great Italian; we spend 3 weeks there and need the pasta fix. We also love Busby's at Oyster Pond. The grilled grouper is just the best.

Leann - D' HERCULE CREOLE My Husband thought it was the best food he had while we were there for 2 weeks. It is down by Mount Vernon on the road across from the medical and PX [near Anse Marcel].

beach bar reviews

W*hether you're looking for a place to while away your day in the sun with an attentive waiter to freshen your daiquiri, or you want to spend the evening under the stars, serenaded by a salsa band, Grand Case has a beach bar to meet your needs.*

beach bars

Just the Facts

Price Level:
$$$

Category:
Beach bar

Meals Served:
Lunch,
Afternoon,
Dinner

Location:
40 Grand Case
Boulevard

Phone:
0590 29 01 85

Website:
calmoscafe.com

Credit Cards:
Visa

Currency:
market rate

Outdoor seating: on beach

Parking:
Nearby lot

Good for:
Groups, Fun

Pros

Tables and lounge chairs right on the beach

Great party atmosphere, without being too loud

Yummy rum drinks; solid burgers
Authentic, fun French waiters

Cons

Slow service when they're busy, which is often; lots of smokers

Calmos Cafe
Overall Rating ★★★★☆

During the first six weeks we spent in Grand Case, we frequented Calmos Cafe more times than I can count. It easily became our favorite spot for a nightcap (or more), as well as a destination to have a casual dinner with friends. We often ran into local residents we had met; it seemed to be a popular meeting place. No reservations required. It's one of two casual cafes situated right on the beach in Grand Case (the other is Zen It, next door). During the day, it's fairly mellow, and at night it heats up considerably, especially as the night wears on and diners from the other restaurants arrive for a nightcap, and particularly on live music nights.

The owners and staff are true Frenchmen, but don't hold that against them: they're in fact quite charming when you get to know them. If you're looking for a high-brow meal of haute cuisine, this isn't your place. But if you're in the mood for a fun, casual, beautiful, laid-back experience...

Food at Calmos Cafe

As beach cafes go, Calmos' food is good. They do a solid burger, and their entrecote (ribeye) is quite succulent. The side dishes aren't amazing. No french fries, instead they have little fried potatoes something like home fries, though they do offer a baked potato or rice as alternatives. I respect that they attempt to offer corn on the cob, one of my favorites, but in this case it is sometimes watery and over-cooked. Overall, the food is decent and not too expensive. However, relative to the other amazing restaurants that you find in Grand Case, if you were looking for a gourmet meal in town, this isn't where you'd go. For lunch, they do have a nice selection of salads and a very solid burger.

When my mom and I camped out there one day during our low season trip, sipping proper cafe au laits while using their free Wifi and watching the frolickers in the water, we were treated to a delicious prosciutto and melon salad, as well as a decent tomato/mozzarella salad. One thing I will say is their salads are generous – we could have easily split one (though what fun would that have been?). In general, it's tough to get a good tomato on St. Martin, even during tomato season, but theirs were fine, and there was a perfect 1:1 ratio between tomato and mozzarella, an important element in my book. They don't skimp on the pesto sauce.

Consumption wise, the highlight of Calmos Cafe is definitely the drinks. They make a tasty, mean rum punch – order the large, and it will have you on your butt in no time

Mood	
Romance	★★★☆☆
Relaxation	★★★★☆
Fun	★★★★★
Family	★★★☆☆
Value	★★★★☆

Food	
Taste	★★★☆☆
Innovation	★★☆☆☆
Display	★★☆☆☆
Drinks	★★★★★

Service	
Attentive	★★★☆☆
Speed	★★★☆☆
Knowledge	★★★☆☆

Atmosphere	
Views	★★★★☆
Decor	★★☆☆☆
Comfort	★★★★☆
Noise	★★★☆☆

flat. They also make their own rums on the roof – literally, on the roof. If you look up, you might catch a glimpse of what you at first think is sun tea, but in reality is flavored rum being brewed as it can only be done in the Caribbean. They have many flavors, up to and including centipede rum, which they display proudly on the bar. I never tried it but friends have. Forget for the moment that centipedes are highly

Prosciutto and melon salad

venomous, and the large ones could kill you... why would you want to drink dead bug? But hey, to each his own. I'm much more a fan of the banana vanilla rum, a relatively common flavor, but Calmos does it best.

On the other hand, I don't recommend the Ti Punch – not because they don't make it properly, but because they do. It's purported to be an island delicacy (not just at Calmos) but my experience was more akin to drinking jet fuel. We weren't that far from the L'Esperance airport, so I

C'est La Vie is the motto

had grounds to wonder. Beyond that, they serve the usual beer suspects, Presidente, Amstel Bright, etc. (no Carib), and they make an extensive menu of frozen drinks. Overall, a solid bar menu.

Service at Calmos Cafe

Calmos, meaning "Be Calm," was opened 14 years ago, and the charming owner Alex bought it eight years ago. For a while it was one of the very few casual restaurants in a sea of gourmet haute cuisine, but in the past six years more casual options have opened up, making Grand Case a more well-rounded destination.

When you dine at Calmos Cafe, you are reminded that St. Martin is in fact a part of France. Alex and all of the waitstaff are French. They work hard trying to keep the many beach diners happy, running around with full trays, but given the cafe's popularity, it's often a while in between ordering and receiving your food/drinks. If you look at this as a place to while away your afternoon or evening on the beach, then this isn't a problem. If you're looking for a quick bite... well... anywhere in the French West Indies, that's a tall order.

Beyond the speed of the service, I will say they also have a French attitude, and I love it. One evening we were enjoying a quiet drink by the water when a group of clearly drunk Americans stumbled in from Mardi (the weekly Tuesday parade event in Grand Case) wearing their Mardi Gras beads, and shamelessly (and loudly) started rearranging chairs to suit their needs. When the waiter arrived, he took one look at them, shrugged, and told them the bar was closed... and then sauntered over to our table and offered us another round.

I'm not entirely sure when the Cafe does officially close... I've malingered there till all hours of the night and never been asked to leave (at least not that I can recall). At the end of your meal, as with most all restaurants in Grand Case, the waiter brings by a bottle of flavored rum with your check and offers you digestif shots. In the case of Calmos, their banana vanilla rum is phenomenally good (I brought back several bottles as gifts). Be sure to offer the waiter a shot as well. If you're good to them, they will sometimes "forget" the bottle at your table.

In general, I will say that after several visits there, we definitely got to know the owner and waiters, and they are a fun group of guys, dedicated to creating an enjoyable environment.

Beware the Ti Punch

If you like your alcohol served raw, with minimal dilution, then Ti Punch, the official drink of St. Martin, is for you... but if you value your liver, I don't recommend it.

Atmosphere at Calmos Cafe

From Grand Case Boulevard, Calmos Cafe doesn't look particularly inviting – you have to navigate an alleyway off the main street, directly opposite the main Grand Case parking lot – but once you enter the bar, you realize why it's a special kind of place. The large bar area is on the sandy beach and out in the open air, but still fully covered. The roof extends over a few large picnic tables and then stops, allowing for several picnic tables and beach chairs scattered along the beach, including right up to the edge of the surf. You can choose a quiet,

Salsa night

Calmos beach

private two-person beach chair experience, looking out over the sea, letting the water lightly lap at your feet. Or, if you're in the mood for a larger party, sit at one of the picnic tables, and join in the fun.

Calmos Cafe is rarely quiet in the evenings, particularly on their live music nights (Thursdays & Sundays), and for the weekly Mardi festivals (Tuesdays) that bring flocks of visitors to all of Grand Case. Their Salsa nights are great fun, and definitely worth going in a group. In general, this is the perfect place to meet up with others, or bring a large bunch of people to enjoy being on a tropical island on a warm winter evening.

Calmos Cafe is completely outside, so you will want to wear bug repellant if you plan to hang out for the evening. They conveniently

share bottles of "Off" at the bar. In fact, if you sit at the bar, you might get sprayed automatically – one night when I was there, the bar started misting at my legs, making me think it was peeing on me. It was in fact a "feature" not a "bug."

During the day, Calmos always has available beach chairs (with proper cushions) and umbrellas, even during high season. They're free if you eat there, which isn't a bad choice. The beach isn't huge but it is quiet and next to a beautiful, calm section of water, perfect for swimming or just bobbing in the mild waves.

The one downside during the day is that every Tues and Fri there are party catamarans that deposit 20-30 day trippers at Calmos for a rum punch lunch. Not only does this large party take over several tables, but they tend to drive the boat directly up in front of the beach, detracting slightly from the view.

In terms of the noise level, though it can get pretty rowdy in the evening, it's surprisingly not too loud on your average night, at least not down by the water. My theory is this is because it's outside and the noise dissipates... of course, you'd have to ask the neighbors how they feel about it. The other thing to note is the amount of smokers. As an American, I have gotten fairly used to never seeing smoking inside anymore. In St. Martin, you frequently see smoking wherever and whenever the person chooses. Given the high percentage of French diners and drinkers at Calmos, there was often a lot of smoking. The good news is because it's open air and on the beach, this isn't much of an issue, with one exception. There is a tempting alcove of couches (just behind the bar, on the street side), and I used to always wonder why people rarely sat there, until I found out first hand. Trust me when I say, you don't want to sit there on a crowded night if you have an issue with smoke.

The prices at Calmos are reasonable, especially relative to the high-end gourmet restaurants down the boulevard. You're much more likely to get out of there for under $100 for two diners with drinks than most other non-lolo restaurants on the boulevard. Given the beautiful beach atmosphere that comes along for the ride, this makes it a great value in my book. Prices are in euros, and they use a general exchange rate to translate to dollars. Sadly, it's not one of the restaurants that offers 1:1 exchange if you pay cash.

If you've ever see the Travel Channel's show "Three Sheets," and the episode they did on St. Martin, you may recognize Calmos Cafe (I was so proud of myself when I realized). It's a great segment on flavored rums, of which Calmos has many.

Bottom Line

Calmos Cafe is our destination of choice for a fun evening under the stars, and not a bad place to go for a quiet, relaxing day on deserted Grand Case beach.

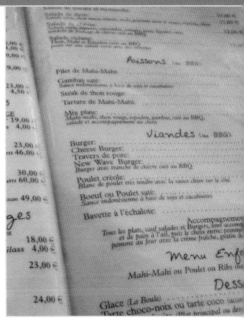

Tasty burgers

Beautiful views

Just the Facts

Price Level:
$$$

Category:
Beach bar

Meals Served:
Breakfast,
Lunch, Dinner

Location:
48 Grand Case
Boulevard

Phone:
0590 87 23 68

Credit Cards:
Visa

Currency:
market rate

*Outdoor
seating:* on
beach

Parking:
Nearby lot

Good for:
Groups, Fun

Pros

Tasty BREAKFAST (in high season)!
Till 11:30! Proper French cafe au
lait!

Comfortable, cushioned beach
chairs and free umbrellas,
uncrowded beach, very
swimmable

Cons

During low season (July - Nov),
Zen It is a shadow of itself: no
breakfast, no iced tea, no
dinner...

Zen It Cafe
Overall Rating ★★★★☆

It took us a little while to find the
best breakfast destination in
Grand Case (or best daytime
beach lounging spot for that
matter), but by week two Steve
and I began frequenting a little
cafe on Boulevard Grand Case
called Zen It. Just next to Calmos
Cafe, they share a beach (and a
credit card machine, and
apparently owners), but for some
reason Zen It is less hectic and
crowded. They have great
cushioned beach chars, and the
requisite umbrellas, and you can
easily move between eating
"indoors" (being that we're in the
Caribbean, there are no doors,
just a roof and floor), and being
out on the beach. But, most
importantly, they do a proper
breakfast that they serve until
11:30, something we had been
desperately seeking.
Unfortunately, they do not serve
breakfast during the low season,
much to my mom's
disappointment on the first
morning of our trip.

Food at Zen It

Not only does Zen It have the best French cafe au lait we've found on the boulevard (I'm amazed at how few places have proper cafe au lait, very disappointed by that), but they do soft-boiled eggs with toast fingers, which I love ("Les Oeufs au Coque," or so I've been led to believe). Their French toast passes Steve's high standards, which is saying something, because the French don't really understand what we Americans call French toast. Their salade nicoise is respectable, even if the tuna isn't a filet, it's the shredded variety. They do a mean croque madame(the ham/cheese sandwich with an egg on top). Their burger is also quite decent, and they do a fresh prosciutto and melon combo. Yes, we spent quite a bit of time on their beach! They also have Wifi (in French, pronounced wee-fee) albeit sporadic and slower than their neighbor's.

We never ate dinner at Zen It, but I will say that they mix some proper drinks, and stay open well into the wee hours. Always a solid beach plan, especially on the nights Calmos is a little too happening.

Atmosphere at Zen It

Even better than the food, Zen It's little stretch of beach is perfect for swimming. The surf is calm, and the beach is perfect, pure, soft sand, unlike the Grand Case Beach Club which was all pebbles (like being in Nice, I wonder if they imported them? it's the only place I've seen a rocky beach here). After a couple mis-starts, I finally got my swimming groove back, and must have gone a full mile, swimming all

the way down to the dive shop mooring, and back to the dinghy docks several times. The water is clear, and with a snorkeling mask on (sans snorkel these days), you can see down to the sandy bottom, probably only ~ 10 feet down. Great conditions for getting over the fear of starring in a movie tag-lined "Jaws, but in the Caribbean."

Mood	
Romance	★★★☆☆
Relaxation	★★★★☆
Fun	★★★★☆
Family	★★★☆☆
Value	★★★★☆

Food	
Taste	★★★★☆
Innovation	★★★☆☆
Display	★★☆☆☆
Drinks	★★★★☆

Service	
Attentive	★★★☆☆
Speed	★★★☆☆
Knowledge	★★★☆☆

Atmosphere	
Views	★★★★★
Decor	★★☆☆☆
Comfort	★★★★☆
Noise	★★★★☆

Warm goat cheese salad

The "inside" of the Zen It restaurant isn't much to speak of, not much more than picnic tables under a hut. On the beach, however, they do have the all-important, properly cushioned beach lounge chairs. And sometimes there is a working bathroom... only sometimes... but there's always the sea.

From the Zen It beach you also have a great view of the prop planes coming in for a landing at Grand Case airport. They fly really

Completely open to the beach

low, right over the Boulevard, and I've been trying desperately to get a proper picture of it. Got a tail, got a nose, but it took a while to time it right to catch the whole plane over the buildings.

Service at Zen It

I think only four people work at Zen It: a cook, two bartenders and one waiter. I wonder that they ever get to sleep since they're there from breakfast through late night. That said, the pace of the restaurant is such that we on occasion saw them taking a break with a quick swim, or joining in a round of shots. I suppose working in St. Martin does have its perks, oui?

We quickly got to know the entire staff, and across the board they are charming French people. Initially I thought they were perhaps a little too charming at times – they love to chat with the patrons, even if someone is waiting for another cafe au lait – but once I embraced "island time," I recognized it as a positive and we got to know them better. I enjoyed practicing my French on them.

Bottom Line

Quieter and more mellow than its next-door cousin Calmos, Zen It was a frequent afternoon beach destination, and occasional evening hang out. More importantly, they serve a proper breakfast during high season, until the vacation-friendly hour of 11:30, and fabulous cafe au lait all day long.

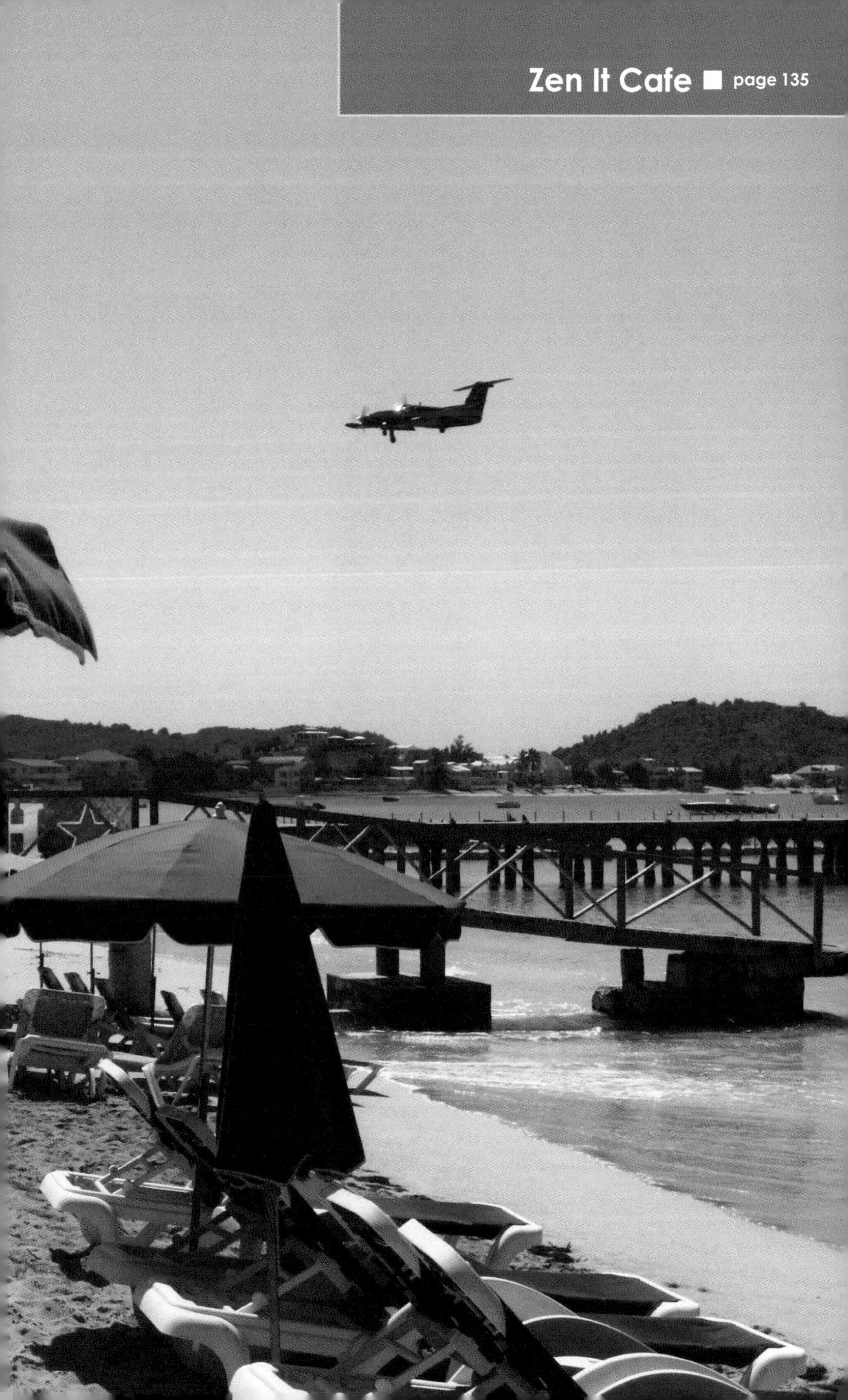

Just the Facts

Price Level:
$$$

Category:
Beach Bar

Meals Served:
Breakfast,
Lunch, Dinner

Location:
Grand Case
Beach Club

Phone:
0590 29 43 90

Website:
grandcasebea
chclub.com

Credit Cards:
Visa

Currency:
market rate

*Outdoor
seating:* on
beach or patio

Parking:
Nearby lot

Good for:
Kids

Pros

Beautiful setting, overlooking the
Grand Case Beach Club, and
convenient if you plan to spend
the day on the beach

Serve decent breakfast, though
only till 10:30

Cons

Out of the way; gated access;
charge for beach chairs

Sunset Cafe
Overall Rating ★★★☆☆

Sunset Cafe is located at the
Grand Case Beach Club hotel
and beach. It's a whole
compound unto itself at the
northern end of Grand Case, up
the "road" past the Tijon
parfumerie (the road is even more
dicey than others you'll have
seen). You have to stop at the
gate to the hotel and ask them to
let you in, but they always do,
albeit sometimes it takes a couple
minutes. The unassuming little
Sunset Cafe serves a decent
breakfast and respectable lunch
in a beautiful outdoor setting.

When you arrive at Sunset Cafe,
you are thrilled to be having
breakfast overlooking the pristine
water, with the sea breeze gently
ruffling your still-wet hair. The
atmosphere is definitely the
upside, even if the breakfast is
only adequate, and what I would
characterize as overly
Americanized. As in, it's what the
French think of as American, and
is almost a caricature of
American cuisine. Lacking other

knowledge or many other options, we went there several times... until the day we arrived at 10:35 to discover they cease breakfast at 10:30. When you're on vacation... well, that's a serious problem in my book.

Food at Sunset Cafe

At breakfast time, Sunset Cafe has decent pastries and fruit. The croissants were respectable, though nothing earth-shattering. The orange juice always comes with ice cubes – something so un-French, but feels like they think Americans want ice cubes, and therefore they include them. I have to say, my biggest disappointment was the lack of proper French cafe au lait. The tea was Lipton, and the coffee was from a large bin. When we ordered the eggs and French toast... well, the omelette was tasty, but other preparations of eggs weren't their forte. The French toast definitely left something to be desired, though as we observed in several instances, this seems to be a generalized misunderstanding by the French of the concept of French toast. It tends to come out more like a fried cake.

My mom ordered the breakfast sandwich on an English muffin, and while it was properly toasted and crispy, with a lovely thin slice of ham, the cheese on top had the distinct bright orange hue that can only have been Kraft American. Like I said, over-Americanized. Even the jam is Smuckers. And the butter is from New Zealand. New Zealand? Why import your butter from around the world when your country makes the best butter anywhere? But I digress.

Mood	
Romance	★★★☆☆
Relaxation	★★★★☆
Fun	★★★☆☆
Family	★★★★☆
Value	★★★☆☆

Food	
Taste	★★★☆☆
Innovation	★★★☆☆
Display	★★★☆☆
Drinks	★★☆☆☆

Service	
Attentive	★★☆☆☆
Speed	★★★☆☆
Knowledge	★★★☆☆

Atmosphere	
Views	★★★★★
Decor	★★★☆☆
Comfort	★★★☆☆
Noise	★★★★☆

At lunch time, we had some tasty offerings; I enjoyed my chicken Creole sandwich quite a bit. Steve's burger was passable, if not earth shattering. I have heard tell of a delightful sliced steak sandwich and frites.

Atmosphere at Sunset Cafe

Atmosphere is definitely why you'll come to Sunset Cafe more than once. Set at the end of Grand Case

Tasty omelette

beach, behind a bluff jutting out into the bay, you have a view of nothing but the Grand Case Beach Club and their beach. There are a couple extremely expensive villas that are just down the beach from the hotel, so all in all, lovely scenery.

What's interesting is that the beach here has its fair share of pebbles, just like in Nice, France. While there is

Open balcony

also sand, the pebbles tend to cluster just at the water break, making entry and dismount somewhat difficult at times. All that said, they have comfortably cushioned beach chairs and umbrellas, and an attendant (with a little flag you can pull so he knows to come help you), which makes this a reasonably nice place to spend a beach day. The beach club also offers floaties, so you can drift in the water just beyond the surf, one of the highlights for me.

The beach club also offers snorkeling and other day excursions, like to Saba and Anguilla. I never partook of their boat excursions but was impressed with the array of what was on offer. Aside from Octopus Diving, this is the place to come in Grand Case if you want to plan a sea-going excursion.

Beyond the beach club, the atmosphere of Sunset Cafe itself is enchanting. It is wide open to the beautiful sea views and breezes, with a roof over part of the restaurant, so you can choose whether you want full air or not. It's a casual, intimate little cafe, perfect for grabbing a glass of wine after an "exhausting" day at the beach.

Service at Sunset Cafe

Aside from having ludicrously short breakfast hours and being turned away, our experience in general with the service at Sunset Cafe was enjoyable. We quickly got to know the waitress we saw several mornings. When we arrived after breakfast closing, she did take pity on us and brought some croissants.

After a few days, we realized the guests at Grand Case Beach Club are on a breakfast-included plan, because when they sat down, they were automatically brought the basic breakfast offering, and then the waitress didn't have to worry about them anymore. As the rare non-hotel guest, that meant we didn't always get much attention, nor do they think to bring you your check; instead you often have to go up to the bar to pay when you're done.

Bottom Line
Though we didn't sample every meal at Sunset Cafe, we found the breakfast to be decent, and heard positive reviews of their other meals. It's conveniently situated as part of the Grand Case Beach Club, making it a good spot to park yourself for an entire day.

View from Sunset Cafe

Fan Favorites - Grand Case Beach Bars
Our Facebook fans like the beach bars in Grand Case:

Connie - We have stayed at the Grand Case everytime we go and we love the breakfast at Sunset Cafe and the view is wonderful also!

Jean-Philippe - What a great place to have a beer, just sitting and looking at the sunset. I love Calmos Café and certainly the beach of Grand-Case. Since visiting the island twice, we have even bought our little paradise StudioMarigot.com

Eve - Calmos is a perennial favorite for us! We'll be back to see them again in April. Love, love, love Grand Case for so many reasons!!

Carole - LOVE Sunset Cafe...we always stay at the Grand Case Beach Club. Great fresh baked breads every morning.

David - My wife and I discovered Calmos last year and loved this place. We saw our first greenflash while enjoying their drinks on the sand. Can not wait till April 2011 so we can visit again.

Fan Favorites - Dutch Beach Bars
Ever heard about watching the planes take off and land? That's at Sunset Bar & Grill in Maho Beach, a destination not to be missed (and not to be confused with Sunset Cafe in Grand Case). Our fans love Sunset Bar & Grill, and a few others on the Dutch side:

Dave - Sunset Beach Bar, Peg Leg Pub and Pineapple Petes are my fav's and in that order

Tessa - Lady of the Sea floating Bar~ Their modo was the Liver is evil and deserve to be punished.... Cheers!

Fan Favorites - Orient Beach

Beyond Grand Case, there's nothing like Orient Beach to find some amazing beach bars. Here are our fans' favorites:

 Mary - Have to say 'Bikini Beach Bar' on Orient Beach. I had a Thai shrimp & scallop dish that you wouldn't expect on the beach. Friendly staff, people & the dog sitting at the bar made my night! Open air with those warm Caribean breezes......

 Candice - Pedro's near the nude beach....they're just fun and it's right a the water....just a fun, relaxing environment! Wish I was there now!!!

 Cheryl - Andy & Cheryl's is the best on the island !!!! At Orient Beach, near the end where you go to the " non-clothing area". Everything on the menu is great!

 Louise - My favorite is Orange Fever. The food is great , the people are so nice, and the prices very reasonable. We ate lunch there almost every day!

 Pat - We were at Orient beach today. We sunbathed in front of La Playa. We had a light lunch there. I had the club sandwich, but Dave's chicken strips looked really good. I had an excellent Merlot.

 Lisa - Tempura shrimp at Bikini Beach is the best shrip I have ever eaten in my life. Nice view too. YUMMY and so not pretentious and unassuming.

 Karen - Palm Beach at Orient is the best, followed by Kaokoe

 Judy - Aloha, Orient Beach. Exceptional Food, funtastic people. Reasonable prices. Have a scrumptious late lunch and play the rest of the day. The first stop once we've get semi unpacked and into swimwear. Kisses to Natalie and Laurie from us.

lolos

lolo reviews

W*e didn't eat at the lolos every day of our trip... but we thought about it. $1 beers. Delicious local BBQ. Perfectly sauteed shrimp Creole. It was hard to walk past the delicious haze of BBQ smoke without wanting to follow your nose... it always knows.*

LUCINDA'S LIST
GUIDEBOOK COMPANY

Just the Facts

Price Level:
$

Category:
BBQ

Meals Served:
Lunch,
Afternoon,
Dinner

Location:
Grand Case
Boulevard

Phone:
0590 51 01 49

Credit Cards:
Don't think so

Currency:
1 $ = 1 euro

*Outdoor
seating:* picnic
tables

Parking:
Nearby lot

Good for:
Everyone!!

Other info:
Open every
day 11 to 11

Pros

Huge plates of delicious food for <
$15, with fantastic hot sauce

$1 Carib beer!

1:1 exchange rate!

Cons

Not the fastest service; next to the
road

Sky's the Limit
Overall Rating ★★★★★

When Steve and I first arrived in
Grand Case, it didn't take us long to
find the lolos. Maybe 5 minutes. See,
you start to walk down Grand Case
Boulevard, and like Toucan Sam says,
"follow your nose, it always knows!"
Very quickly you'll smell the BBQ, and
see the wisps of smoke, and find
yourself in lolo heaven: cheap, tasty,
satisfying, heavenly food.

The thing is... there are four lolos all
clustered together. How do you know
which one is the best? It's almost
impossible to distinguish where one
ends and the next begins. Their
menus are practically identical, as
are the smells and picnic tables
(albeit sometimes there is a different
paint color). We played eenie-
meenie-miny-mo a couple times
before we got smart and asked the
locals. After all... who better to know
the lolos than the locals?

The answer? Clear. Unequivocal.
Sky's the Limit. They'll tell you that
there are some who say "Talk of the

Town" is your best bet, and don't get me wrong, it's fantastic in its own right, but when you walk by on a boisterous Saturday night, it's Sky's the Limit that clamors with local slang.

Food at Sky's the Limit

If you've never been to a lolo, let me start by explaining that it's all about the BBQ. Ribs. Chicken. Lobster. Fish. Shrimp. It would seem all it takes to start a lolo is to salvage an ancient 50-gallon steel drum cut in half and filled with charcoal, lay in an endless supply of paper plates, et voila! Oh, and a fridge full to the brim with Carib, the island beer of choice. Add in some startlingly, shockingly tasty side dishes, and you are in business.

So we started to go to Sky's the Limit, and wow, there is just nothing like it. No matter what you order, the trick is to order it as "Food." Shrimp Food. Rib Food. Lobster Food. What that means at Sky's the Limit is that you want all that and a bag of crisps. The fully monty. The whole shebang. Whichever main dish you have selected, it will arrive laden with friends galore: rice and beans like you've never tasted; cole slaw and potato salad that is perfectly drenched in "extra heavy" mayonnaise and some unknown variety of island crack; macaroni and cheese and spaghetti, oddly complementary; and a tiny green salad comprised of a single, lonely leaf of lettuce and three or four shreds of carrot, just to make you feel virtuous. Oh, and a fried plantain thrown into the mix, just for good measure.

On our first visit, I was appalled at the amount of food, and vowed to

Mood	
Romance	★★☆☆☆
Relaxation	★★★☆☆
Fun	★★★★☆
Family	★★★★☆
Value	★★★★★

Food	
Taste	★★★★★
Innovation	★★★☆☆
Display	★★★☆☆
Drinks	★★★★☆

Service	
Attentive	★★☆☆☆
Speed	★★☆☆☆
Knowledge	★★★☆☆

Atmosphere	
Views	★☆☆☆☆
Decor	★☆☆☆☆
Comfort	★★☆☆☆
Noise	★★☆☆☆

eat only half... only to find myself mere minutes later practically licking my plate clean. It was like I

Local's Choice

Locals swear by Sky's the Limit. Once we tried it, we never went anywhere else.

Rib food

was in a trance. Once you start, you can't stop; there is no moderation at the lolos. The insane thing is that everything goes well together. It's not about each individual taste. Don't go all Howard Hughes. The

Playful service

more you mix it up, the better. Odd, but true.

Now, a word about the condiments. Use with *abandon* AND *caution.* Matouk's hot sauce, in all flavors, will rock your world. If there is no label, be even more afraid. My approach is to blend it with the rice and beans to defuse the deadly heat, leaving the flavor you will come to love. Mixed into the shrimp sauce... OMG.

Over the course of our first six-week trip, we must have eaten at Sky's the Limit at least a dozen times. Lunch, dinner, mid-day snack... if we were crispy from the sun and needing sustenance, Sky's the Limit was at hand. During this time, our order rarely varied: Shrimp Food (for me) and Rib Food (for Steve). Oh, and about half a dozen Carib. Did I mention the beers are $1 each? You really can't not order one at that price.

Having now tasted Shrimp Food at several lolos and other places around the island, I can say that Sky's the Limit is the best (with the one notable exception of Alain at the Hotel L'Esplanade pool bar).

When I returned to Sky's the Limit with my mom, it was our third lolo of the trip, and I intentionally left it till the last day. It did not disappoint. Grey Squirrel was just as pleased with Sky's the Limit as I was, and after unabashedly scarfing down her Rib Food, whole-heartedly agreed it deserved its loyal following.

Service at Sky's the Limit
In my many visits to Sky's the Limit, I will say that every one of the

people we have met there has been charming and hard-working. However, that does not necessarily translate into what Americans consider to be top-notch service. These ladies work their butts off, but it is pretty much always busy, and so are they. But it's more than just busy. The fact is, these ladies know everyone (remember this is the locals' fave?). So the upside is they fully engage with you. The downside is they fully engage with everyone else too, so your turn may be a little slow in coming. Whether you sit roadside or closer to the kitchen, it doesn't necessarily help. The trick is to order a couple of Carib right off the bat, and your afternoon will slip by in a delicious haze.

Atmosphere at Sky's the Limit

As I've mentioned, the lolos are all packed into one area in Grand Case. Though Sky's the Limit isn't one of the ones overlooking the beach and water - it's right on the road - I think this makes them work even harder at their food. But it means the ambiance is somewhat saturated with the smell and sounds of gasoline. It's also chock-full of locals, especially on Sundays - I've noticed Sunday is a particularly popular day for local families to head to the lolos - so it may be pretty crowded. This is a good sign. But it means that if you're in a hurry, you might be tempted to try another one. If so, Talk of the Town is your next best bet. I don't recommend Rib Shack #6, despite their proximity to the water.

Bottom Line

You hear about the famous lolos on St. Martin, and Sky's the Limit is the

Open BBQ

best I've found. Less than $15 for a huge, tasty, satisfying meal. $1 Carib beers. Fun, island atmosphere. You really must experience it on your trip, or you haven't been to the island... and I might have to confiscate your SXM souvenir t-shirt.

Hubby squirrel

Just the Facts

Price Level:
$

Category:
BBQ

Meals Served:
Lunch,
Afternoon,
Dinner

Location:
Grand Case
Boulevard

Phone:
0590 52 84 93

Credit Cards:
Don't think so

Currency:
1 $ = 1 euro

*Outdoor
seating:* picnic
tables

Parking:
Nearby lot

Good for:
Everyone!!

Other info:
Open every
day 11 to 11

Pros

Half the locals swear by it

Crazy cheap with fabulous,
satisfying, tasty local food

1:1 exchange rate!

Cons

Not the fastest service, but the
best Lolos never are

Talk of the Town
Overall Rating ★★★★☆

Of all the lolos, after Sky's the Limit,
you hear the most talk about Talk of
the Town. It would seem that most
regulars are evenly split in their
loyalties, and once you pick, you
don't cross the picket line. Though
we've been loyal followers of Sky's
the Limit for many, many satisfying
meals, we put on our secret squirrel
disguises and went undercover in
the interest of research.

In fact, my mom and I hit Talk of the
Town minutes after arriving in St.
Martin. I had taken a hideous
redeye, followed by a three-hour
layover in Charlotte, followed by
another four-hour flight – 12 hours of
travel time in all. My mom had been
told to arrive at the Dulles airport at
5am, even though they don't open
till 5:30am. When we hit Hotel
L'Esplanade at 3pm, we were tired,
hungry and bitter, and in need of a
life-saving infusion of island BBQ.

Food at Talk of the Town
After months of deprivation, I
obviously had to order the crevettes

Creole, otherwise known as shrimp Creole. At Talk of the Town, you get two side orders with your main dish (unless you order a la carte, which you can), and so I of course chose the red beans & rice and potato salad, just to be sure I got the full dosage of life-saving island nectar. It was tough to choose between the potato salad and cole slaw, but what can you do? My mom opted for the BBQ chicken, which I had never had, having been hooked on the shrimp crack early in my last visit.

When the shrimp arrived, I was a little leery. I had forgotten the radioactive hue of orange that accompanies the Creole sauce. Moreover, the red beans and rice had a slight brown tinge. And yet, I was utterly starving, not to mention deprived of island cuisine, so I trusted my instincts and went for it. The shrimp were delicious. Larger than I have seen elsewhere, and properly doused in a healthy helping of garlicky saucy goodness. The rice and beans tasted exactly as I remembered from the lolos despite the darker color. I rooted through the condiments basket for the Matouk Creole hot sauce, and carefully mixed in a small helping to the rice and beans, ensuring it would augment the flavor without causing a coronary.

My mom tore into her BBQ chicken with gusto. After several attempts to use the fork/knife, she finally gave into the island vibe, and started to pick it apart with her fingers, properly embracing her inner carnivore. After my mom saw me add the hot sauce, she poured a generous serving directly on top of her chicken. I tried to warn her. Mistakes were made. Prices were

Mood

Romance	★★☆☆☆
Relaxation	★★★☆☆
Fun	★★★★☆
Family	★★★★☆
Value	★★★★★

Food

Taste	★★★★☆
Innovation	★★☆☆☆
Display	★★☆☆☆
Drinks	★★★★☆

Service

Attentive	★★☆☆☆
Speed	★★☆☆☆
Knowledge	★★☆☆☆

Atmosphere

Views	★☆☆☆☆
Decor	★☆☆☆☆
Comfort	★★☆☆☆
Noise	★★☆☆☆

paid. Tears ensued. And eventually she regained the power of speech enough to say how good her meal was. So a note of caution. Tread carefully with the island hot sauce until you have built up your tolerance.

Service at Talk of the Town

Let's be clear, you don't go to any of the lolos because you expect great service, you go because it's a worries. Once you get over your fear of being rude, and realize you can request things from any of the waitresses, your meal experience gets a lot better.

The best news at the lolos is that it's always 1 euro = 1 dollar when you pay cash. Oh, and it's impossible to spend more than $30 on a meal including several drinks, unless you pony up for the lobster, in which case, well, sky's the limit.

Picnic table atmosphere

delicious meal for a crazy cheap price. Once we got their attention to place our orders, it wasn't too long before the food arrived, but after that... not so much. It would seem we bumped right into the 4pm shift change, because our waitress grabbed her purse and walked off somewhere in between my first and second Carib. No

Happy Grey Squirrel

Atmosphere at Talk of the Town
All four of the lolos in Grand Case share the same area. There's not a whole lot of difference in the picnic tables at each one. Nor is there much difference in the lively bantering of the locals. Even if you speak French, or think you do, you are unlikely to understand the slang they're throwing at each other, but you can tell it's funny and probably rude, no matter the language. The atmosphere of the lolos is casually perfect regardless of whether you're dripping wet and covered in sand, or freshly showered and planning to go out on the town after dinner. Anything goes.

Bottom line
Some of the lolos are more cheap than good, but not this one. Talk of the Town is deserving of its loyal following. If something ever happened to Sky's the Limit, I know I could count on Talk of the Town to save me.

Fan Favorites - Lolos

Our Facebook fans have some distinct opinions about the Lolos, both in Grand Case and the rest of the island. Here's what they had to say:

Judie - Talk of the Town is better than Sky's the Limit in my opinion. The christophens are to die for. Anyone go to Chez Yvettes? Love the johnny cakes.

Talayah - They are both just OK, and last time I went to Talk of the Town, they overcharged us (they had one price for locals and another for tourists), so this summer I went to Sky's the Limit. If you're thinking inexpensive, there's a BBQ place called Lido in Simpson Bay - just a hut, but good chicken & ribs. I also like to venture out a bit for local food. There's a new restaurant in the middle region, Honey's under the Tamarind. I tried that this summer. Meanwhile, there's also Johnny B's Under the Tree (it's been years since I've been and I hear it is now more commercialized) in Cole Bay and LongAcre's by the Rock, both on the Dutch side. Both basically shacks, but good food and low prices.

Nancy - first meal is always lee's roadside grill, across from the royal palm, simpson bay....great ribs, great price and easy to get a table.....live music and dancing, as well...

Danielle - Johnny's Under the Tree, Philipsburg

Juanita - Still like Captain Frenchys in Grand Case - amazing fresh seafood... the meal was 11 bucks and worth 25 simply loved it! He even opened his doors when we came back a second time. He was going fishing to supply his LoLo and stopped and made our food!"

Cindy - Ate there [Talk of the Town] the week before last! The food was awesome and the prices were great!! love that place! Took lots of pictures there too!! :)

Maureen - Talk of the Town!! We had the best lobster ever!!

Fan Favorites - Lolos

Carole - Lolos r the best! When in St. Maarten make sure to visit the Lady C floating bar. Nice people and lots of fun!

Caren - Love. Love, Love the lolo's!!! They are always the best places!

Deborah - OK You've convinced me. We stay in Maho but we always take a day trip to Grand Case so we can eat at Talk of the Town. But after reading you article I am definitely going to go to Sky's the Limit. It better be as good as you say OR I will be looking for you.....LOL. Never had lobster at Talk of the Town just the chicken and ribs. I'll have to try the lobster next time.

David - We make sure we eat at either at least once while we're there.

Mario - Not to be a downer, but Talk of the Town, Too was not as good this June as it was last June. The floor under our table was coated with an oily film and the food was a disappointment. Friends of ours had similar experiences. We'll go back next year to see how they and Sky's the Limit are doing. Hopefully, just a temporary glitch. (Best pizza is Villa Pizza in Cul de Sac.)

Lynnie - My good friend, Emil Lake's, place [Sky's the Limit] met him in 1982 !! Please give him big kiss and hug!!!

Sandy -We always stop by Lee's Roadside Grill twice while we are on the island; once for ribs and once for their fresh grilled grouper! Yum...

Arlene - Sky's The Limit you can try all the local foods (lots of different flavours) everything is fresh fish, shrimp, whole lobster all done on the grill, always busy and great staff. Can't wait to be back in February.

hotels, activities, etc.

*T*hough we're all about food when we're in Grand Case, that doesn't mean there aren't other things to do and see. From diving and snorkeling to wine tasting and perfume-making, there's more to Grand Case than just amazing restaurants.

LUCINDA'S LIST
GUIDEBOOK COMPANY

hotels, activities, etc.

Hotel L'Esplanade
Overall Rating ★★★★★

Price Level:
$$$$

Category:
Luxury Boutique

Amenities:
Views, Pool,
Restaurant,
Balconies

Location:
Rte. de
l'Esperance

Phone:
0590 87 06 55
866 596 8365

Website:
lesplanade.co
m

Credit Cards:
Visa, Amex

Currency:
U.S. Dollars

Parking:
on site

Other info:
- They do
laundry

- Continental
breakfast

Pros

Beautiful, large, well-appointed
and comfortable rooms

Small, intimate hotel with great
staff

Perfect location in Grand Case,
St. Martin, short walk to 30+
restaurants

Cons

Not on the beach; no spa on site;
no room service except
continental breakfast

We spent six weeks at the Hotel L'Esplanade on our first trip. As our introduction to St. Martin, it couldn't have been better, and inspired us to uproot our lives and focus on spending as much time there as possible. Across the board it gets the highest marks. When I returned in August with my mom, there was no question of going anywhere else, we simply had to return "home" to Hotel L'Esplanade.

The hotel is tucked away on a small hill overlooking the bay of Grand Case. With classic, inviting architecture and amazing views from every vantage point, it is perfectly situated to take advantage of its surroundings. It has only 24 rooms, arranged on two floors, and every room has a patio/balcony and view of the ocean.

When we arrived and walked down to the office, we were greeted warmly by the staff, who wasted no time in helping us get comfortably settled in our spacious, bright, well-appointed room. There aren't any bellmen, just the multi-purpose office staff who will help with everything and anything that is needed. As soon as we entered the room, we breathed a huge sigh, and settled into our new home.

Rooms at the Hotel L'Esplanade

How to describe the rooms? Amazing. Perfect. Phenomenal. We spent six weeks in the same room and never felt claustrophobic or in need of a change. As another guest said, it's like being at home, without all the work!

The rooms are very large with beautifully detailed dark wood accents. Our first room was an oversized loft (980 square feet), and it included fully-equipped kitchen, two balconies, living room and 1 1/2 baths. It had two floors, with soaring ceilings, making it feel even more spacious than its actual square footage.

Upstairs in the bedroom area (who gets to have *stairs* in a hotel room?!?), the bed was a huge king-size four poster, romantically draped with mosquito netting. The bed was amazingly comfortable and inviting, piled high with high-thread-count linens, duvet and pillows in pristine white. My husband is a huge fan of having a pile of feather pillows. There's a ceiling fan and screens on the balcony doors, so you can choose to go tropical if you wish, but the central air conditioning works quietly and effectively. If you leave the curtains open, you can wake up to views of the bay from your bed... or you can close the curtains and create a welcoming cocoon to sleep in undisturbed.

Mood

Romance	★★★★★
Relaxation	★★★★★
Fun	★★★☆☆
Family	★★☆☆☆
Value	★★★★☆

Rooms

Size	★★★★★
Furniture	★★★★★
Web/TV	★★★★☆
Patio	★★★★★

Service

Front desk	★★★★★
Maids	★★★★★
Bar	★★★★★

Amenities

Pool	★★★★☆
Beach	★★★☆☆
Restaurant	★★★☆☆
Convenience	★★★★☆

Important Bug Note: you only need to close the mosquito net around the bed when your husband forgets to close the screen door while he's photographing the sunset from the balcony, at which point it's critical. Otherwise we never, ever saw uninvited critters in our room.

The living room had a proper, comfortable couch - none of that flimsy wicker crap you see in so

Oversized loft upstairs

channels, and the media cabinet had a DVD player and an iPod docking station. There was an internet connection... though it's sadly not Wi-Fi. They provide you with an extra-long network cable, which isn't the best if you're an internet-intensive family like us, but gets the job done. They also provided us with an industrial strength transformer for all our electronics charging needs, both critical and a nice touch.

The bathroom was reasonably sized, though not palatial, and we had to get used to the French shower - there's no shower curtain and the hot/cold are flipped on the dial - but for all that, it was perfectly good. I had imported all manner of toiletries with me for our long trip, which I almost regretted when I saw they not only provided high quality soaps and lotions from Provence, but they were thoughtful enough to give us full size amenities for our long stay. There was also a half-bath on the first floor which definitely came in handy.

many tropical hotels that makes you want to sit on the floor - and the rest of the furniture was beautiful Balinese wood. Clearly the owners put a lot of thought into the decor: it's tasteful and high-end. The TV got a whole slew of NY cable channels, including movie

There are several sizes of rooms: studios, lofts, oversized lofts (which we were in), and 1-bedrooms. During our first stay, we became friends with other guests, and got to see one of the 1-bedrooms. This is important - the 1-bedrooms and loft rooms are nicer than most NY apartments I've seen, so you can actually invite friends over without that awkward feeling that they're going to have to sit on your bed. What a treat on vacation to not feel claustrophobic in your room.

Oversized loft downstairs

On our second trip, I went with my mom and decided the 1-bedroom would work out better to provide

some privacy. The 1-bedroom is slightly larger at 1020 square feet, and has a more open living area and better kitchen, renovated and open to the dining area. The only downside is it doesn't have the striking double-tall ceilings and windows of the lofts, though it still has the wide open feeling of a wall of windows overlooking the spectacular view. The bathroom was also fantastic, beautifully and recently renovated - HUGE double shower, two sinks, tons of drawers and storage space. There was only one balcony, but because it curved around, it had similar furniture and surface area to the two balconies of the loft put together. The furniture inside and out was just as comfortable and high quality as the loft, as was the decor.

Storage space in both the loft and the 1-bedroom was excellent. There aren't dressers per se, instead they have huge closets with shelves and hangers. They also have a dirty laundry basket, which for some reason was huge for me - such a cheap item, and yet so many hotels don't provide such homey conveniences. There's also a rack where you can hang your wet bathing suit to dry, convenient when you're living in it. In the loft, there was even a huge storage closet under the stairs where we stored our many suitcases and snorkeling equipment, another convenient feature.

The 1-bedroom room was on the first floor of the hotel, which meant we had to go down a flight of stairs to get to it, and it meant we had upstairs neighbors. However, we never ever heard anything. In fact, in the loft, in the 1-bedroom, in the

One-bedroom living room

eight weeks total that I spent there, I never heard other guests through the walls/ceiling... except once, when some poor drunk stumbled into his table in the dark and had some loud, choice things to say about it.

Patio

Sunset from room #5

Going back, would I choose an oversized loft versus a 1-bedroom? Hard to say, they're both fabulous rooms, and you really can't go wrong. The loft feels more open and airy with its double-tall, arched ceilings, but the downside is you can hear your husband when he gets up early and goes downstairs to practice his "French" with the computer while you're trying to sleep. The 1-bedroom provides a handy door for the late sleeper.

Of course, I haven't been in every single one of the 24 rooms, so your mileage may vary, but the ones I have been in, I was exceedingly impressed.

The view, oh, the view! Every night we took pictures of the spectacular sunsets over Grand Case Bay; you just can't help yourself when surrounded by such incredible beauty. You get photography OCD, I swear you simply can't sit there without taking pictures. Though the balconies are stacked on top of each other, and if you stand at a particular angle you can see your neighbors' balcony, it was architected such that you generally felt completely secluded and didn't even hear each other. Even with two stories of windows, no one can ever see into your room. Ever. It's perfect privacy. There was both a table with chairs, perfect for eating breakfast basking in the warm morning, as well as two comfortable steamer lounge chairs, perfect for sipping your rum digestif while watching the stars. We spent many evenings on our balcony.

Service at the Hotel L'Esplanade

The entire staff at Hotel L'Esplanade was beyond pleasant and attentive. These guys really do understand what it means to be customer-centric. Everyone was so incredibly welcoming and helpful, always there to help with whatever you need.

Housekeeping learned our habits and never bothered us in the mornings; if we left really late in the day, we hung the "please service" sign and they always took care of it immediately. Even if we were only gone an hour, the room was pristine when we returned. We never had an early morning knock, nor did we ever come home to find the room unclean because we went out later in the day, both of which are huge pet peeves of mine. And every time we did return, the room was simply spotless - sandy beach towels replaced with a neat stack of clean ones, and not a single speck of sand anywhere.

The staff at the front desk - Myriam, Anna, Philomena - all happily did anything and everything we asked, and always followed up to make sure it met our expectations and needs. They took the time to get to know us during our stay, making us feel like we were a part of the family. If they recommend a restaurant, they really want to know if it was all you had hoped so they can continue to provide good advice to other guests. They arranged wonderful in-room massages for us - same day even. Breakfast was always impeccably on time, and they never scoffed at us if we answered the door in our bathrobes, hair askew. They will do laundry for you for a very reasonable fee ($20/load instead of per shirt), and it's back in your room folded by the end of the day, another little perk that sets them apart from so many hotels. There is not a single thing to complain about. The first time we tried to rent a DVD we couldn't find the remote, and therefore couldn't switch it to English from French (and didn't quite feel up to watching "The Hurt Locker" en Francais); within an hour of calling the front desk, they had brought us a completely new DVD player, with remote.

Amenities at the Hotel L'Esplanade

Before our first trip, I read complaints that L'Esplanade doesn't have a large pool. To those people I simply say: you're crazy. No, you won't be doing long laps, nor is it a resort-style pool with water slides and hot tubs, but it is perfectly sized for the hotel and the space. We never lacked for a place to comfortably lounge, or shade from

Pool

Path to Grand Case

take days for them to lose their city edge, but inevitably Alain had them happily fed and sipping on rum drinks, discovering their freewheeling island personas, before they could blink a travel-weary eye.

Try Alain's shrimp and the grilled grouper for lunch - both are amazing. My husband also swears by the burger and fries if you're longing for home. Alain officially closes up shop at 6pm so you have to find yourself another location for dinner and evening drinks (though on occasion he has been known to make an exception)... luckily there are 30+ amazing restaurants an easy five-minute walk down the hill.

During low season the pool bar is closed, so no tasty lunches or swim up drinks. However, the upside was there were several afternoons when my mom and I literally had the entire pool to ourselves for hours on end (except the occasional errant gecko of course). Complete tranquility.

Because Hotel L'Esplanade is small, it doesn't have an on-site spa. This is probably the only feature that I missed while we were there. There aren't any spas in all of Grand Case as far as I could tell (Le Shore advertises one, but when I inquired, I was told it won't be open until "next year"). The staff did kindly book us in-room massages that were enjoyable, but I admit that I missed basking in a spa's facilities. I recognize it's a natural trade-off between a small hotel and a larger resort with a spa; I'll take the boutique hotel all day long since I can drive to a spa.

One last, very important note - we were lucky enough to meet the owners of L'Esplanade while we

either a large umbrella or the indigenous foliage, nor was the pool itself ever too crowded for a good float. It's also lovingly decorated with tile, reminiscent of a chateau in Provence, France. In addition, it was an intimate gathering spot for all the guests - you really got to know people in a wonderfully casual environment. We met some fabulous people at the pool, many of whom have been coming back year after year for longer than they could remember.

During the day at the pool you'll also find Alain, a masterful chef and mixologist (not to mention master of festivities). Every day at 4:30 we watched newbies stumble in, fresh from the plane, bright white legs shimmering beneath suitcase-pressed khaki shorts. You'd look at these new arrivals and think it will were there. They are truly wonderful people who put their heart and passion into their hotel, and it shows. It's evident in every aspect of the experience staying at their hotel - you feel like you've been invited to your friends' beautiful home, and you never want to leave.

Convenience of the Hotel L'Esplanade

I had some concern about the lack of beachfront location when we booked. Originally we thought perhaps we'd switch it up in the middle of our stay and move to Le Petit Hotel, their sister property on the beach. But no. The location is in fact perfect. You are a 5-minute stumble, I mean walk, down to the thick of Grand Case restaurants, beach, lolos, bars, everything you could possibly want... without being in the middle of the madness. We walked the path at all hours of day and night and never had any issues; it's well-lit and tended. There's even a sweet little chicken named "Miss Plucky" who hangs out at the bottom of the path, in front of the very cool pottery store. Be sure to stop in - Cecile's pottery makes for a worthy souvenir.

Bottom Line

When I went back for a second trip to St. Martin, I asked myself whether in the interest of research I should branch out and try other hotels... and the answer was an emphatic NO. I don't know why we would ever stay anywhere else. Though Hotel L'Esplanade isn't the least expensive option, it is an incredible value because of the quality of room, service, location and overall experience. You will not be disappointed with your stay.

Pool, looking at hotel

Octopus Diving
Overall Rating ★★★★★

During the six weeks we stayed in Grand Case, I went on five different dives with Octopus Diving. I simply never saw any reason to go with anyone else.

They run two boats a day, at 8am and 1pm... and take note, these are not "island" times. The boat leaves on time, so be on time. They often go local in Grand Case Bay, to Creole Rock and Turtle Reef (appropriately named), or else head out to Tintamarre or around to the Dutch side. They are very flexible about destination – if there is somewhere particular you want to go, they will often accommodate – but most importantly they assess the conditions that day to determine the best destination. If they're going local, they will take snorkelers as well. Either way, they are very cognizant of crowd control, and never take more than a handful at a time. During high season, I could usually get a spot on the boat within a few days, but it's always good to call ahead if

Just the Facts

Price Level:
$$$

Activity Type:
Diving & Snorkeling

Location:
15 Grand Case Boulevard

Phone:
0590 29 11 27

Website:
octopusdiving.com

Credit Cards:
Visa

Currency:
market rate

Parking:
Nearby lot

Other info:
- Boats leave promptly at 8 a.m. and 1 p.m. daily
- 10% off for Lucinda's List fans!

Pros

Knowledgeable, passionate divemasters who always make sure you have a great dive

Never more than six divers

Fast catamaran and high quality equipment

Cons

Sometimes visit the same spots, so discuss destinations if going out multiple times with them you want to go to a particular place.

Price & Value at Octopus Diving

The prices for snorkel and dive excursions at Octopus are in line with other shops: $40 for a snorkel trip, $99 for a 2-tank dive with all equipment included. Even if you're not certified and have never dived before, they offer a "discovery" dive for $99 for one site, $149 for two. This is a great way to decide if you want to go for your certification, or just to check it out.

Most importantly, the value you get for your money is huge. These guys genuinely care whether or not you're going to have a good experience, from start to finish. Scheduling my dives couldn't have been easier or more pleasant. No matter when I would go by the dive shop, whoever was working was incredibly helpful.

They are all exceptionally knowledgeable about the many dive sites around the island, but more importantly, they tell it like it is.

Mood	
Romance	★★★★☆
Relaxation	★★★☆☆
Fun	★★★★★
Family	★★★★☆
Value	★★★★★

Quality	
Experience	★★★★☆
Service	★★★☆☆
Amenities	★★★☆☆

When I ask how the visibility is, I know I'm going to get a straight up answer. They'll tell me when I should wait a couple days, versus when it's great. How often do you hear that? They're not just trying to fill up their boat.

These guys love to dive themselves, and they treat all their customers

Octopussy

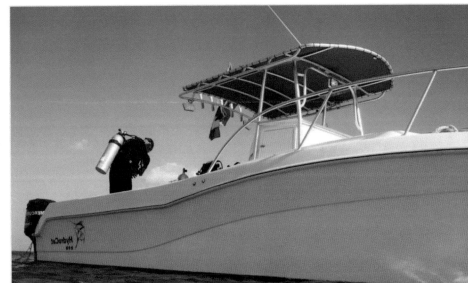

Divemaster Stu

divemasters Stu and Aure, and their two divemaster interns Jenn and Mark, I just never had a bad dive. Every one of them is a passionate diver, which makes them phenomenal divemasters.

For Chris and Sally, this is clearly a labor of love. Not only do they know their dive sites like the back of their hand (including sites no one else visits), they genuinely love what they do, and it shows. On one dive we even went out exploring a new reef. They have fun, and create a relaxed – and safe – environment for you to enjoy yourself.

When it comes to dealing with all the equipment, they are the picture of efficiency. And let's be clear, you don't have to carry or worry about a thing.

These guys know where to go and when to go. They know the turtles by name, and know where to find all the cool critters. There have never been more than five other divers when I've gone (and often fewer), and because of that, they can really engage with you and show you around, and point out things you might have missed otherwise. I've seen eagle rays, sting rays, sleeping nurse sharks, turtles, eels, huge lobster, underwater caves... the list goes on.

Most importantly, these guys are just good people; they genuinely care. The first dive I went on with them, I got a little panicky, not having been diving in several years. They were the picture of patience, and took care of me until I was comfortable again. When one of the women on a dive started to feel seasick, we took her to Tintamarre beach in between dives so she

the way they want to be treated. From what I've heard from people who have trained with them, this translates into their certification programs as well; they genuinely want to make sure you learn what you need to know to have a safe and fun experience that will get you hooked on diving for life.

Service at Octopus Diving

All I can say is I'm blown away. Over the course of my five dives, I went out with pretty much everyone who was working at the shop at the time. Between the two owners Chris and Sally, and the two

Sally (owner)

could recover without having to sit on a rocking boat.

Atmosphere at Octopus Diving

The Octopus dive shop is an unassuming little hole in the wall on Grand Case Boulevard, but don't let that fool you. They have a surprisingly decent selection of accessories if you want to rent or purchase snorkel or dive equipment. They'll even let you test out a mask before you buy or rent it.

Most importantly for a dive operation, they have a fast, comfortable double-hulled catamaran (named "Octopussy," of course) that they use for all their excursions. It's specifically geared to be easy to get on/off the boat with all your equipment. It's parked (moored) right across the street, so there's no long trek out to the dock. There are never more than a handful of divers or snorkelers on the trip, so you never feel packed onto the boat. There are always plenty of bottles of water and fruit to get you through the day. These guys just run a high-class operation that doesn't skimp.

Bottom line

Every person I've met at this small shop genuinely loves what they do, and cares about ensuring everyone who steps on their boat has a phenomenal experience. This is a great place to dive. Whether you've been on a hundred dives or are a complete novice, Octopus takes great care of you.

Oh, and if you are experienced and wondering if it's worth diving in St. Martin at all? The answer is a resounding yes!

Eagle ray

Turtles galore

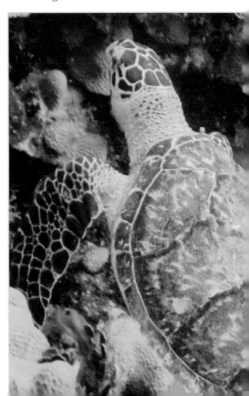

Shopping

Can't We Just Eat In?

Eating out every night, especially for a longer trip, just doesn't make sense. And, for that matter, you probably want to have some snacks back in the room, just in case. We found that there are several grocery shopping options that made sense, depending on how much you wanted to spend, how far you were willing to go and how authentic you wanted.

US Supermarche, Grand Case

The funny thing about U.S. Supermarche is that it is a consummately French grocery experience... named "U.S." Ah, how I love the French ironic sense of humor. It's a large grocery store with all the requisite items: freshly baked goods, local rums, meats (the entrecote, also known as ribeye, proved exceptionally tasty), pastas, sunscreen, bug repellant, and all the other usual grocery items. Not to mention packaged French yummies that you won't find in the U.S.: pre-made thin-crust pizzas, incredible steak au poivre and hollandaise sauces in magical little vacuum-packed cases, eradiated milk (and therefore room temperature) and a typically ridonculous selection of cheeses, salamis and French wine.

The U.S. Market isn't in downtown Grand Case - it's a short drive past the airport, located in a large industrial park. I wouldn't suggest walking it, but it's a quick drive. My one suggestion is that if it's during the day, buy your wine from Bacchus, located just behind the U.S. Market. Note: the U.S. Market is open until 8 p.m. during the week, but Sundays it closes at 2 p.m., so get there early. Also, it gets very crowded around 6:30 or 7, around the time when everyone else decides to cook at home as well. It's also on the pricey side. This isn't the place for bargains.

Le Bounty, Grand Case, St. Martin

If you're staying in Grand Case, but lack a car, have no fear! Le Bounty is there to help you out. Located just off the Grand Case Boulevard (turn at Bistrot Caraibes), next to Crousti, the only proper boulangerie in Grand Case, Le Bounty is a surprisingly good little market. You pay for the convenience, of course, but it's an easy walk and has everything from breakfast cereal and chips to a decent selection of cheeses, wine and fish. Like I said, a surprising collection for such a small store. Don't bother with the L'Epicerie, located on Grand Case Boulevard, unless all you need is a six-pack of Carib.

Marigot Market

If you manage to get out of bed early enough on a Wednesday or

Saturday (i.e. before 1 p.m.), you can hit the Marigot market. We never got there early enough to experience the outdoor fresh seafood market, but our friend Alain at the Hotel L'Esplanade pool certainly fed us enough of the items he procured there, and I can personally vouch for the tasty freshness of the grouper, shrimp and mussels. We did manage to hit the market in time for the fresh produce, and the packaged spices and hot sauces, and those were definitely worth the trip. Look for the merchants under the permanent white roofs. The fair in the market square is more crafts-oriented, (some would say tchotchkes), and that goes on every day.

Le Grande Marche, Philipsburg or Cole Bay

The irony of the Grande Marche, a more French name than U.S. Market, is that it's a far more Americanized shopping experience and located on the Dutch side of St. Maarten. Just barely. When we first heard that you could get much better deals on groceries if you schlepped to the Dutch side, it seemed so far away, but if you go at the right time, it's a quick 15-minute jaunt from Grand Case. When I say the right time, I mean avoid the middle of the day when the drawbridge in Philipsburg goes up and snarls traffic around the entire island. Seriously. But I digress. The other serious benefit of heading to Le Grande Marche, aside from much better prices, is that the one in Cole Bay is located next to the nearest U.S. Dollar-dispensing ATM to French St. Martin. You won't get dollars in French St. Martin. This is directly over the border, so the closest spot. Note: on Sundays it's

Marigot market

often tapped out, so don't wait till you get desperate.

Where's the Bread???

If you've spent any time in France in your life - and let's just call it like we see it, and if you're of the female persuasion - the first thing you want to find when you arrive in a French-speaking destination is the nearest Chocolate Croissant. I mean, would life be worth living without them? And you know, every town in

Sarafina's (Marigot)

Crousti, the Grand Case Boulangerie

France, no matter how small, has a boulangerie where a desperate woman can procure herself said delicacy, not to mention fresh, crusty, warm, buttery baguettes for those times when the chocolate just seems to decadent.

In the case of Grand Case, you'll be concerned when you don't see a boulangerie on the main Boulevard, but take heart - Crousti is just around the corner! Yes, that's it's actual name. French humor. But I

Bacchus wine store

digress. Crousti is not only one of the few places that is air conditioned in the town, it has lovely baguettes, croissants, cinnamon twirls - these I HIGHLY recommend, by the way - and even prepared sandwiches, little pizzas, quiches, basically anything you might need for a little snack. The boulangerie is a must see. Turn off the Boulevard next to Bistrot Caraibes, and it's on your right.

Note: if you are heading to Marigot, I STRONGLY advise you to stop at Sarafina's Boulangerie. It is simply out of this world. The assortment of pastry delicacies warms the cockles of my heart... and if you ever need a cake or tart, look no further.

Did Someone Say WINE?

Just behind the U.S. Market in Grand Case, in a random, unobtrusive industrial park, you will find the mecca of wine stores: Bacchus. I've been to amazing wine stores in Paris, in California, in NY... amateurs, all of them! At first glance, the incredible selection of 2600 wines from all over the world might feel overwhelming. But stay strong... and be nice to the kind gentleman who offers to help you. After I ineptly described what I like, Stephan introduced me to several of my new favorite best friends, ahem, wines, and they were surprisingly reasonable. Bacchus was one of my first stops on my return trip with my mother... and it wasn't my last. Oh, and did I mention they are one of my all-time favorite places for lunch? You'll feel your arteries hardening while you read the menu, but rest assured, it is worth it. They even have shrink-wrapped gourmet treats, perfect for a picnic at the beach.

Souvenirs Galore

As with all tropical destinations, Grand Case has its fair share of opportunities to purchase souvenirs. There is "Sexy Fruits," an oddly named but lovely little boutique with t-shirts, jewelry and other locally made items that make for great gifts. "C'est La Vie" is the Calmos Cafe motto and their boutique name; great t-shirts, not great prices. There's a small art gallery and a tattoo parlor. In general, you'll find no shortage of t-shirts, bathing suits and cover-ups. But if you're looking for designer boutiques, head to Marigot or Philipsburg.

French Pharmacies? Ooh La La

You might be reading this, thinking to yourself, why do I care where the pharmacy is? Well, let me tell you. French pharmacies are wondrous places. Think the first floor of Bloomingdale's or Barney's - cosmetics, high-end sunscreen and glorious French toiletries galore. My mom and I spent hours in there one day, browsing and testing. Oh, and you can also get the usual stuff like cough drops... not to mention those items the French government has seen fit to approve for over-the-counter that the U.S. government has not. I'm not encouraging anything... just saying.

The Grand Case Pharmacy is located not on the Grand Case Boulevard but on the main thoroughfare that goes just inland of Grand Case. Right next door is your closest ATM (euros only).

Smells Good...

If the Pharmacy isn't your speed, Grand Case also has its own

Grand Case Pharmacy

French-style parfumerie. This is not your average Caribbean activity! Perfect on a rainy day, or when you're feeling a little too crispy, you can head to Tijon to peruse their scents and skincare products. Or, you can go all-in, and take their perfume-making class to design your very own signature scent. Alas, I never could convince my husband of the necessity of this activity, and lucky for us it didn't rain that often. However, I have heard very positive reviews from other travelers. Worth checking out.

Bottom Line

Though Grand Case is known for its culinary attractions, there is more to this small town than initially meets the eye. Be sure to explore it fully.

Acknowledgements

I am deeply indebted to the many people who have helped me with this book. Madam J has been my eyes and ears on the ground, contributing two fantastic reviews along with her intrepid dinner companion, Marc Au Marc. Kristin and Marc have become amazing friends and exceptional contributors.

My mother, Vicki, a.k.a. Grey Squirrel... this book wouldn't exist without her indomitable travel spirit and editing skills. Of course I have to thank my father Jack for letting his wife go galavanting in the Caribbean for two weeks without him. My 25,000 Facebook fans' tips, questions, stories, photos, responses, and everything in between, help remind me every day why I love St. Martin.

Last, but in no way least, I owe an enormous debt of gratitude to my husband Steve, without who's technical and design skills this book would resemble a child's coloring book (and not a pretty one at that)... and most importantly, without who's love and support I would be utterly lost.

LUCINDA'S LIST
GUIDEBOOK COMPANY

Made in the USA
Lexington, KY
07 March 2014